Library of
Davidson College

THEOLOGICAL REFLECTIONS ON THE CHARISMATIC RENEWAL

Proceedings of the
Chicago Conference
October 1-2, 1976

Edited by
John C. Haughey, S.J.

SERVANT BOOKS
Ann Arbor, Michigan

copyright © 1978 Servant Books

Published by: Servant Books
P.O. Box 8617
Ann Arbor, Michigan 48107

Available from: Servant Publications
Distribution Center
237 North Michigan
South Bend, Indiana 46601

Scripture quotations in the articles by Haughey, Sullivan, and
  Yocum are taken from:
   The Revised Standard Version Bible
   Copyrighted 1946, 1952, © 1971, 1973 by the Division
   of Christian Education of the National Council of the
   Churches of Christ in the U.S.A., and used by permission.

Scripture quotations in the article by Stuhlmueller are taken
  from:
   The New American Bible
   Copyright © 1970 by the Confraternity of Christian
   Doctrine, Washington, D.C., and used by permission
   of copyright owner. All rights reserved.

Printed in the United States of America.

ISBN 0-89283-048-4

CONTENTS

    Preface
    Kevin Ranaghan   vii

I.   The Charismatic Renewal
    and Biblical Hermeneutics
    Francis Martin   1

    Response
    Carroll Stuhlmueller, C.P.   39

II.   New Aspects of
    Spiritual Direction
    Ernest E. Larkin, O.Carm.   43

    Response
    Robert L. Faricy, S.J.   69
    Response
    Judith C. Tydings   73

III.   The Role of Tradition
    Francis A. Sullivan, S.J.   79

    Response
    Richard M. Liddy   95

IV.   The Relationship Between
    Charismatic Authority
    and Church Office
    John C. Haughey, S.J.   99

    Response
    Bruce Yocum   125

CONTRIBUTORS

Robert L. Faricy, S.J. is professor of spiritual theology at the Gregorian University in Rome, and professor of philosophy at the Collegio S. Roberto Bellarmino, also in Rome.

John C. Haughey, S.J. is research associate at the Woodstock Theological Center, Washington, D.C., and a corresponding editor of *America* magazine.

Ernest E. Larkin, O.Carm is professor of spiritual theology at the Kino Institute, Phoenix, Arizona.

Richard M. Liddy is professor of philosophy at Immaculate Conception Seminary, Darlington, New Jersey.

Francis Martin is a doctoral candidate in sacred scripture at the Ecole Biblique in Jerusalem, and a member of the Madonna House Apostolate, Combermere, Ontario.

Kevin Ranaghan is a coordinator of the People of Praise community, South Bend, Indiana, and a permanent deacon of the diocese of Fort Wayne–South Bend.

Carroll Stuhlmueller, C.P. is professor of scripture at the Catholic Theological Union, Chicago, Illinois.

Francis A. Sullivan, S.J. is professor of dogmatic theology at the Gregorian University in Rome.

Judith C. Tydings is a coordinator of the Mother of God community, Potomac, Maryland.

Bruce Yocum is a coordinator of the Word of God community, Ann Arbor, Michigan.

PREFACE

The Church has traditionally referred to the enterprise of theology as "faith seeking understanding." God's word touches us. We believe. We count ourselves among God's people. The theologian reflects upon this experience of faith and seeks to understand it. From the time of St. Paul, the Church has regarded this form of inquiry as an important part of its life.

Today, the charismatic renewal, in particular, has attracted the attention of theologians both for its character as a powerful action of God in the lives of individuals, and for the richness of its contribution to the whole Church. Indeed, we can all attest to the activity of the Holy Spirit in and through this renewal. Many people have become Christians or have experienced a significant deepening of their faith through their involvement in the charismatic renewal. Most of them have experienced the operation of charisms or spiritual gifts—tongues, prophecy, teaching, and others—which existed in the early Church. They have experienced a new desire to pray, a greater thirst for scripture, and the guidance of the Holy Spirit. Many of them have wanted to commit their lives more fully to God and other brothers and sisters through membership in Christian communities. The charismatic renewal has added a fresh evangelical thrust to the life of God's people, a movement of the Spirit that promises to have lasting ecumenical significance.

The four theologians whose work is collected in this volume utilize the methods and resources of their discipline in attempting to evaluate the "data" that forms so large a part of the daily experience of those involved in the charismatic renewal. Their papers examine four diverse but nonetheless related topics. In his paper, "The Charismatic Renewal and Biblical Hermeneutics," Francis Martin addresses a basic theological question in its application to our experience of the charismatic renewal and in its relationship to selected aspects of St. Paul's use of the word *soma*. In "New Aspects of Spiritual Direction," Ernest Larkin examines a pastoral issue in the charismatic renewal in the light of Church history. Francis Sullivan takes up the question of the role of Tradition in his paper by the same title, a topic which has lately attracted considerable interest. John Haughey explores the relationship between charismatic authority and church office. Also included here are the responses of five conference participants to individual papers, responses by Robert Faricy, Richard Liddy, Carroll Stuhlmueller, Judith Tydings, and Bruce Yocum.

These papers are the proceedings of a theological conference that was sponsored by the National Service Committee of the Catholic Charismatic Renewal in October 1976 at Chicago, Illinois. By its charter, the National Service Committee seeks to foster the charismatic renewal in the Church and of the Church, and takes an active concern to bring professional theological reflection to bear upon this renewal. I feel that these four papers—and the responses to them—fulfill this objective of the National Service Committee and are representative of the contributions of modern theology to the charismatic renewal.

Kevin Ranaghan, Ph.D.

THE CHARISMATIC RENEWAL AND BIBLICAL HERMENEUTICS

Francis Martin

Hermeneutics and Experience

Some Preliminary Reflections

The goal this study sets for itself is quite modest. It wishes first to discuss the relation between hermeneutics and experience, and then apply the results of that discussion to our experience of the charismatic renewal. It will then proceed to apply the results of the first discussion to the relationship of the charismatic renewal to certain aspects of St. Paul's teaching on *soma*.[1] One of the firm convictions of this study is that the charismatic renewal offers a very fruitful ground for the cultivation and modification of hermeneutical methods precisely because it is a faith experience. We will seek to penetrate more deeply into the meaning of this faith experience in the light of some of the normative prophetic teaching of the NT, and, correlatively, we will seek to understand more accurately some of the Pauline "anthropological" teaching in the light of this experience.

One of the most vexing problems in modern biblical study today is what is gently called the "hermeneutical gap." There is an ever-widening space separating the exegete's attempt to understand the text in itself, and his capacity to show his contemporaries the meaning of that text within the context of their actual experiences.[2]

Walter Wink has not hesitated to describe the situation as

one of "bankruptcy," justifying his epithet by observing that it is not a question of whether or not a given institution is functioning well, but simply whether or not it is profitable.[3] Paul Dreyfus has begun a series of articles in which he contrasts exegesis *en Sorbonne* and exegesis *en Eglise*.[4] Frederick Herzog[5] has pointed out that the very horizon of the exegete, interested as he is in the preservation of the "establishment" within whose overall structure he is maintained as a professor, is foreign to the horizon of the authors of the New Testament. Herzog observes that some of the New Testament authors were poor men themselves, and that all of them addressed people not many of whom "were wise in the ordinary sense of the word, or were influential people or came from noble families" (1Cor 1,26) and for whom "the world as we know it is passing away" (1Cor 7,31).

There have been many sincere attempts to bridge this hermeneutical gap, and it should be stated at the outset that much of the disgruntled commentary on modern exegesis done by preachers and other pious folk helps not at all. What we are faced with in the Church is not a crisis of exegesis, but a crisis of faith; and in this we are all equally involved and equally responsible.

On the level of the scientific functioning of the theological disciplines, we are confronted with the necessity of what Thomas Kuhn aptly calls a "scientific revolution," by which he means "a non-cumulative, developmental episode(s) in which an older paradigm is replaced in whole or in part by an incompatible new one."[6] If we attempt a general definition of "paradigm," based on the twenty-one or so uses of the term in Kuhn's work,[7] we could say that a paradigm is a pre-existing mental framework constructed on the basis of expressed or unexpressed philosophical presuppositions within which data can be coherently organized, related, and rendered meaningful. It is a "mind set."

In modern exegesis, our basic paradigm has been constructed out of the material of the "referential" disciplines. That is, the text is interpreted by referring it to its textual, philological, historical, cultural, literary, and theological *milieux*. These procedures are valid as far as they go, since they are searching for relationship, and all meaning is the perception of relation. Difficulty arises, however, when one moves from referential exegesis to referential hermeneutics, that is, from the meaning of the text in relation to *its* environment, to the meaning of the text in relation to *our* environment.[8]

The modern statement of this problem was elaborated, as is well known, by Dilthey and Hegel; in this century, efforts to come to grips with this challenge are associated with names such as Bultmann, Fuchs, Ebeling, Robinson, and, in a larger context, those of Heidegger, Lonergan, and especially Ricoeur and Gadamer.[9] The surest acquisition of these studies has been the clear realization that the interpreter approaches the text with a "prior understanding" or "pre-existing horizon," or, if you will, a paradigm which conditions what he will see and how he will see it. In the words of N. R. Hanson, "All data are theory laden."[10]

Because exegesis purports to be the interpretation of a message composed in one horizon and received in another,[11] exegesis itself ought to be seen as being hermeneutic. In order for exegesis to actually take on a more hermeneutical dimension, it is necessary that a greater conscious awareness be achieved of the interpreter's investigative horizon and that the area of the coalescence of the two horizons be defined in terms of some principle of continuity.[12] A truly successful exegesis, therefore, would be one in which the gap between the meaning discerned by the exegete on the one hand, and the reason why the text has meaning for his contemporaries, on the other, will be closed by essentially the same thing that closes the gap between the exegete and his text.

Attempts have been made to elaborate the fundamental and overarching nature of this "gap-closer" or principle of continuity. New Testament exegesis, in particular, has sought for this in terms of "self-understanding" (Bultmann), and in the unique performative function of faith-language in the *kerygma* (Fuchs, Ebeling). More recently, this principle of continuity has been looked for in the common archetypes present in the human psyche (Wink), and in the communality of the deep structures of communication (structuralism). All of these attempts seek to go beyond referential interpretation, which is restricted to the milieu of the text, and aspire to perform a true hermeneutical function in mediating a meaning, a perception of relationship, between the message of the text and the receivers of the text today.

In this kind of exgesis, the historical disciplines have a unique role to play in assuring a self-conscious awareness and respect for the original textual horizon. Of course, the text must be treated as more than an "object." It is not enough to describe, in phenomenological terms, *what* the text is saying. An interpretation is not the same as the description of an object; it is the re-presentation of an act of communication in such a way that what is said is heard and perceived as having meaning.[13]

It is precisely in the development of a more hermeneutical emphasis in exegesis that I see the role of the charismatic renewal. As a faith experience, the charismatic renewal provides the essential principle of continuity by which there can be a genuine coalescence of horizons between the authors of the NT, and those who receive their message today.

A Discussion of the Hermeneutic Circle

The description of the process by which a new experience should give rise to a new confrontation with the sacred text has been well delineated by Juan Luis Segundo in his latest work, *The Liberation of Theology*. Segundo first lists two preconditions for a productive "hermeneutic circle": (1) profound and enriching questions and suspicions about our real situation; (2) a new interpretation of the Bible that is equally profound and enriching. There are, Segundo goes on to add, four decisive factors in this circle:

> *Firstly,* there is our way of experiencing reality, which leads us to ideological suspicion. *Secondly,* there is the application of our ideological suspicion to the whole ideological superstructure in general and to theology in particular. *Thirdly,* there comes a new way of experiencing theological reality that leads us to exegetical suspicion, that is to the suspicion that the prevailing interpretation of the Bible has not taken important pieces of data into account. *Fourthly,* we have our new hermeneutic, that is, our new way of interpreting the fountainhead of our faith (i.e., Scripture) with the new elements at our disposal.[14]

The starting point of this excellent description is found precisely in "our way" of experiencing. Segundo, who is seeking to establish a basic methodology for the theology of liberation, will quite rightly insist that the Latin American experience highlights an appalling dissonance between the dignity of man and the actual life of men —whether oppressed or oppressor— within the "Christian" context of the social, political, and economic frameworks of Latin America. This is basically a faith experience for a believer like Segundo, even though the word of God which one can hear in such a situation is a word of divine pathos:[15] the pain of God in the suffering of man.

There are other faith experiences as well, both modern and ancient, which have provided the basis for "ideological suspicion" of the status quo. Regardless of whether or not they were professional theologians, all the saints achieved an "interpretation by sympathy," since they were reading the sacred text "in the spirit in which it was written."[16]

Not all of these interpretations were genuine exegeses, however. Concentrating as they did on the text as "means" rather than "object," our predecessors often ignored what I have called the "referential" aspect of exegesis. Just as frequently, they were prevented from acquiring this type of understanding due to the limited nature of their scientific tools. In their treatment of scripture, it is the *strength* of the interpreter's horizon which upsets the delicate reciprocity between the message of the text and the pre-understanding of the receiver. The role of the historical disciplines in preserving a balanced perspective is therefore an important one. I would like to illustrate these points with a criticism of Segundo's example of a completed hermeneutical circle.[17]

Segundo presents four cases where attempts were made to construct a hermeneutical circle. He begins with a quotation from Karl Mannheim, who is describing the first step in such an undertaking: the criticism of experience.

> Karl Mannheim writes: 'An increasing number of concrete cases makes it evident that (a) every formulation of a problem is made possible by a *previous actual human experience* which involves such a problem; (b) in selection from the multiplicity of data there is involved an *act of will* on the part of the knower; and (c) forces arising out of living experience are significant in the *direction which the treatment of the problem* follows.'[18]

These words, which anticipate some of Kuhn's assertions, are then applied by Segundo to the efforts of Harvey Cox, Karl Marx, Max Weber, and James Cone to construct a hermeneutical circle. We see here that Cox never finishes the first step of this process. He never arrives at "ideological suspicion" because he lacks its essential ingredient as defined by Mannheim, that is, he does not make an "act of the will." Marx does not apply his suspicion to the total ideological superstructure, since he simply eliminates, rather than suspects, religion. Weber did reach the third stage, that of an explicitly exegetical suspicion, but he does not carry through to a new way of interpreting scripture.

The example given by Segundo of a completed hermeneutical circle is that of James Cone in his work, *A Black Theology of Liberation*. There is an act of the will, which leads to ideological suspicion and a "selection from the multiplicity of data"; and this two-fold rhythm is repeated in an exegetical suspicion and a new hermeneutic that restricts itself to the application of biblical data to the question of black liberation.

I do not doubt that Cone achieves the closing of the hermeneutical circle, nor that his book has been of valuable service to American attempts to rehear the word of God. However, I do maintain that Cone's study is not a true *biblical* hermeneutics. The context created by the act of the will in restricting the multiplicity of data has forced the word of God into a horizon which does not respect that of its original transmitters.[19] In place of an "objective exegesis" that contents itself with describing the assertions made by a particular text, we have a "subjective hermeneutics" that forces the message of the Bible into a pre-understanding that has arbitrarily chosen to ignore data that could modify the interpretation. Though the intention is more urgent, and the message more important than that contained in our old theology manuals, the methodological error is the same: in place of a coalescence of horizons, there is a plundering of the Bible for "proof texts."

The analysis of Segundo is a useful aid in structuring a hermeneutical process that begins with faith experience. His is a true theological methodology: *fides* (faith experience) *quaerens intellectum* (understanding in the light of transmitted revelation).

The difficulty I have expressed refers to the functioning of this approach, not its basis. We are speaking of a circular *process* when we speak of the hermeneutical circle: it is a delicate and reciprocal activity by which two faith experiences stimulate, modify, and shed light on one another. The process begins with a faith judgment—I would say a prophetic judgment—regarding contemporary experience; endowed with this horizon, we must seek enlightenment, modification, and confirmation in the word of God; and this in turn more sharply focuses our faith understanding of what we experience.[20] Unless the process is reciprocal, the result is either an irrelevant exercise in textual analysis or an arbitrary consultation of the sources of revelation exclusively in the light of immediate preoccupations.

Let us move on now to a consideration of the charismatic renewal as a faith experience, attempting to isolate some of its features and make them the starting point of a hermeneutical circle.

The Charismatic Renewal as Faith Experience and Anthropology

Modern Attempts to Understand Man

I would like to propose here the hypothesis that the area of theology which the charismatic renewal has rendered most subject to "ideological suspicion" is that of anthropology. We are beginning to experience, though still in a very feeble manner, a prophetic judgment on our modern view of man. The charismatic renewal is spearheading and pointing beyond itself to what is best in the modern philosophical and theological revolt against the view of man prevailing in our culture. What we are living is a word to all men. In the light of faith experience and the word of God, some of the best of modern man's uneasiness and discontent with himself is being confirmed and purified.

Two of the most recent studies in theological anthropology, those of Pannenberg and Moltmann, rely heavily on a basic insight that was propounded by Herder in his study on the origin of language and developed by Max Scheler in his *Man's Place in Nature*.[21] These thinkers have insisted that man's existence is characterized by "openness to the world." By the very fact that man does not possess an extremely refined set of specialized senses, he is not confined to that process of sensient selectivity which characterizes animals whose exceptionally sensitive faculties of perception can operate only in relation to those things that are necessary for the perpetuation of the individual and the species.

> Only man generally experiences objects—in the precise sense of the word—as independent entities that stand opposite him, that are strange, and that can evoke astonishment. It is specifically human to pause curiously over things and to be taken by their strangeness and uniqueness in almost breathless interest.[22]

But this "openness to the world" includes more than objects. The basic interaction that a person has with reality is his interaction with another person. Just as the appreciation that man can perceive and relate to objects (an "I-it" relation) is a safeguard against the mechanistic and behavioristic theories of man, so too the fact that man's fundamental relationships are with other human beings, and this precisely in their non-object reality (an "I-thou" relation), protects him from being treated and manipulated as nothing more than a component in a field of force, whether this force be economic, military, or political.

The revolt of religious anthropology against the views and systems which stultify man's radical and insatiable openness to what is beyond him is reflected in other revolts within the fields of philosophical, cultural, and sociological anthropology. I would like, in this regard, to make some remarks about one aspect of what some modern thinkers are saying concerning the human body, since it is this aspect of anthropology that will most concern us for the remainder of this study.

Any system that considers man primarily as an object rather than a subject basically reduces man to the status of a spatiocorporeal entity. The philosophies underlying the political systems of the extreme right and the extreme left have this view in common, as, for example, the critiques of Marcuse,[23] Marcel[24], and Ellul[25] have variously shown. Whenever man's destiny is identified with absorption into the powers of the state, we have the blasphemy of emperor worship, and the cult of the gods who maintain political, economic, and cosmic security. It was their refusal to enter into this form of subtle and overt manipulation, and its religious expression, that led to the execution of the first Christians as "atheists," a charge nowadays usually termed "disloyalty" to the existing left or right-wing group in power.

When man is simply a body among other useful objects, he is sooner or later "one-dimensioned." On the other hand, when man despises or tries to ignore his bodily reality, he falls victim to anxiety and schizophrenic self-indulgence. The Gnosticism, legalism, Manichaeism, and other forms of intellectual magic, of which we have both ancient and modern examples, illustrate this convincingly. One of the great contributions made by Teilhard de Chardin to Christian thought was the restoration of a faith understanding of man's vocation as a child of God, in the context of his continuity with the cosmos.

Other branches of science have also begun to express their dissatisfaction with our basic paradigm of the human body. Let me give two brief examples, one from the sociology of medicine, the other from sociological anthropology. Both of these concern the relationship between our perception of body, and society.

In the sociology of medicine, historical, cultural, and transcultural studies have indicated the intimate relationship existing between a person's view of himself in his bodily existence, and the societal views and expectations surrounding him. Parsons was the first to study the "sick role" in our society, and his work has been carried on, notably by Rodney Coe. Coe diagrams the various aspects of that role, pointing out that "the sick role provides a means for legitimating the temporary non-performance of a sick member and to minimize the disruption in the role performance of other members of the group."[26]

Our very perceptions of ourselves as sick involve a particular view of our bodily reality, and this we learn from our society. Since our body has become an "object" even to ourselves, we look upon the recovering of health in much the same way that we consider the resumed good functioning of a repaired machine. Though in recent years we are prepared to see some sort of mutual causality being exercised by the psyche and the *soma,* we have yet to appreciate the role of our environment in our perception of our health.

Recently, Horacio Fabrega published his "Study of Medical Problems in Preliterate Settings." Among his conclusions he states:

> ... studying medical phenomena in preliterate settings enables the testing of hypotheses dealing with medical concerns that have been generated in Western industralized settings. Diseases are ubiquitous, as are man's attempts to deal with them. Our knowledge about disease correlates, however, as we have emphasized throughout this report, contains many of our cultural biases.[27]

Thus, modern studies are beginning to uncover our "biases": those processes of "selective inattention" latent in our very understanding of the relationship between our health and sickness. Some of these insights are valuable in understanding the connection between the true significance of healing, and social justice, as this is being experienced in the charismatic renewal.[28]

A very clear and forceful confirmation of this view of the relation between body and society can be found in the work of

Mary Douglas in the fields of religious and sociological anthropology. She summarily resumes some of her own insights into the concepts of "purity and danger" in a more recent study entitled "Social Preconditions of Enthusiasm and Heterodoxy." She makes the following statement:

> Doctrines which use the human body as their metaphor, including those which define the relation of spirit to flesh, are likely to be especially concerned with social relationships . . . I would maintain that the human body is never seen as a body without at the same time being treated as an image of society. Or, to put it differently, there is no natural way of considering the body which does not take account of the social dimension.[29]

This intimate correlation between body and society will be verified in the Pauline concept of *soma*. However, before bringing our newly acquired ideological suspicion into confrontation with the word of God, we must first attempt to see this modern rediscovery in terms of the faith experience of the charismatic renewal and the prophetic judgment it brings to bear.

The Charismatic Renewal as a Word about Man

We have just considered some of the many converging attempts to understand man in his corporeity as something other than an isolated monad. We have also seen that our modern "objective consciousness" affects the way we think of ourselves, and thus of others, both in regard to the experiences of "health" and "sickness" and in our consciousness of how we relate to society. Theologians too have begun to say that "The body is man's 'primordial activity' (G. Siewerth), the 'symbolic reality' of man (K. Rahner), his 'medium of being' (B. Welte), in which he lives and 'is there' and is present . . ."[30]

Our experience of the charismatic renewal has come to show us once again that, in Tertullian's famous phrase, "The flesh is the hinge of salvation."[31] The essential characteristic of the charismatic renewal is that it is an *experience,* a style of consciousness, a conscious assimilation of the reality of the good news in Jesus Christ. It is in this, first and foremost, that our anthropology is challenged. How can we situate such an experience within the paradigm of the *res extensa* and *res cogitans* of Descartes, or the Freudian and other models which view man as a fragile equilibrium, poised between a drive toward pleasure or power and opposing elements deriving from assimilated behavior patterns? The charismatic renewal is quite simply an act of God in the Church, renewing the mystery of Pentecost, and calling us to new depths of faith and a new judgment regarding the nature of our life in Christ. It is in this light that we must bring to bear a prophetic understanding on the "joys and the hopes, the griefs and the anxieties of men of this age"[32] whose attempts to understand themselves, as we have seen, are moving toward a deeper grasp of what it means to be open to the world, to men, and to God.

It is extremely difficult to describe an experience or even to define what an experience is. Jean Mouroux defines religious experience as "the act—or group of acts—through which man becomes aware of himself in relation to God."[33] What is most characteristic of the charismatic religious experience is its corporeal nature. The exercise of the charisms themselves demands a totally human kind of activity, whether we consider tongues, prophecy, and healing, or whether we turn our attention to the deep gifts of prayer, in common or in private, whose various relationships to the body were commonly studied in our treatises on prayer;[34] or whether we consider those gifts of leadership and shepherding by which the community is governed. God's Spirit has erupted into our lives. He has conferred upon us a deeper sense of oneness with ourselves, thus repairing the fragmentation imposed upon us by our experience of society. He has also given us the possibility of deep and meaningful intersubjective communication with the Trinity and with other human beings, the effect of which has been to break through the isolation of our self-enclosed egos. Once again the Lord has crowned the *preparatio evangelica* brought about by all those who have sought for a real meaning in human life. What we are experiencing in the charismatic renewal is a renewed action of God in the body of believers, and this is giving us courage to look to the Lord for understanding of what it means to be human. Once again, words such as these bold phrases of Cyril of Alexandria are making sense to us:

> The mystery of Christ is therefore the beginning and the way whereby we have become sharers of the Spirit, and united with God. All are sanctified with him in this manner.
>
> Since we too were united and fused, as it were, with God and with one another, although we are with our soul and body separate and distinct persons, the Only-Begotten has devised a means worthy of his wisdom and of the Father's counsel.
>
> In one body, his own, he blesses (and transforms) in mystic communion the faithful who believe in him, and makes them 'con-corporeal' with him and among themselves.
>
> Who can divide them? Who could deprive them of their physical union, when they are bound together in unity with Christ by means of his holy body?[35]

The charismatic renewal has restored to us this faith experience of our identity, especially in the area of communal living. This has pointed the way to a prophetic understanding of all that we have been groping for in our re-understanding of ourselves, and has led us to the word of God for confirmation and enlightenment.

Some Aspects of the Pauline Concept of Soma

General Usage

While not overlooking the work of others in this field,[36] we should consider ourselves fortunate in having two recent studies which have done much toward clarifying the background of Paul's anthropological terminology and the uniqueness of his own contribution. I am referring to the work of Robert Jewett, *Paul's Anthropological Terms: A Study of Their Use in Conflict Settings,*[37] and that of Robert Gundry, *Soma in Biblical Theology, with Emphasis on Pauline Anthropology.*[38] Despite their divergence in outlook and preoccupation, these two works serve to complement one another and can be used profitably, though cautiously.[39]

The work of Jewett is particularly helpful in tracing the component factors operative in Paul's use of *soma,* as well as delineating Paul's unique creative insights.[40] Both aspects of the question are very important for the present study, since Paul was faced with the same sort of *preparatio evangelica* that we face today. By the grace given him in his experience of Christ, he was able to judge and perfect, with prophetic authority, the view of man prevalent in his age. Through the appreciation of each of these aspects, we will deepen and purify the word we hear today in our experience of the charismatic renewal in the context of the search for a more adequate understanding of man.

We will restrict our discussion to the eight letters generally considered to be of direct Pauline authorship: the two Thessalonian letters, Galatians, Philippians, what we have now as 1 and 2 Corinthians,[41] Philemon, and Romans. We will leave aside questions regarding Paul's degree of responsibility for Colossians and Ephesians, since most of the points we wish to raise are not affected by the doctrine in these two later letters.

We may distinguish three aspects of the word *soma* in the eight letters we have just enumerated. First of all, there is a nontechnical use available to men in nearly every language (though not Hebrew) by which they refer to the common experience of themselves and others as being of a particular material configuration.[42] We will treat of this general usage here, and then in the next section consider Paul's unique contribution to the notion of *soma*.

We should bear in mind that Paul's ordinary or nontechnical usage does not correspond to our objectified use of the term today, but more nearly to the concept of the body as the "symbolic reality" of man or as his concrete mode of realizing his relationships and expressing his society. This potential of *soma* is exploited by Paul and given a new faith context, even in what we are calling here his general usage.

Sometimes Paul uses *soma* as he uses *sarx,* as one element in his traditional Jewish view of man as flesh/body and spirit: thus, 1Cor 7,34; 2Cor 7,1; 4,11 (see Phlm 16). [43]

Once, either because it was an established liturgical formula, or a common usage at Thessalonica, or because he wanted to correct a gnostic misunderstanding, Paul expresses his desire that the God of peace sanctify the Thessalonians wholly, and that their "spirit and soul and body be kept complete and unblemished at the parousia of our Lord Jesus Christ" (1Thes 5,23).[44]

At other times, Paul's view of *soma* as the vehicle of communion and the basis of relationship seems to be further deepened by his faith view of that relationship. Thus in Gal 6,17, Paul speaks of his scars as being the stigmata of Jesus which he bears in his body; just as in Phil 1,20 he desires that Christ be magnified in his body either through death or through life. This faith view of the corporeal basis for relationships is also present in 1Cor 7,4 when Paul speaks of the mutual and equal rights that man and wife possess in regard to the *soma* of their partner: "For the woman does not have power over her own body, rather the man; and likewise *(omoios)* the man does not have power over his own body, rather the woman." Given the principles laid down in the preceding section (1Cor 6,12-20) we should, most probably, see here an application of the fact that "Your bodies are the members of Christ" (1Cor 6,15). We should appreciate the equality accorded by Paul to men and women in Christ, regarding their relationships as body-persons, and not just bodies.

There are some negative uses of the term *soma* as well, many of which are comprehensible only if we bear in mind what has been said about the body as the basis for relationships. Thus in Rom 7,24, after Paul describes the plight of Adam and therefore of all men,[45] he asks, "Who will deliver me from the body of this death?" This must mean, "Who will deliver me from this aspect of my personality by which I perpetuate the kind of relation to this world that leads to separation from God?"

Actually, the usual Pauline word for this "earthly sphere which becomes the source of sin when man places his trust in it"[46] is *sarx*, a word which, though it can have a neutral connotation (for example, Gal 2,20), is, unlike *soma*, rarely used to portray man capable of new life. Instead, it often depicts man as unredeemed, turned-in on himself, and resisting the presence of the new age.

Soma may have been used in Rom 7,24 in order to accentuate the ambiguity of the human situation: man is capable of relationship to the sphere that leads to death, but he is delivered by "the law of the Spirit of life in Christ Jesus from the law of sin and of death" (Rom 8,2).

Soma is also described as "dead because of sin" and "mortal" in Rom 8,10-11. I understand *soma*, rather than *sarx*, to be used in the second case because the term "body" lends itself to being considered the object of the "life-giving" action of God, and is itself the underlying substratum which passes from death to life. It is not clear to me why Paul would speak of the body as dead on account of sin unless, as Jewett maintains, *soma* is substituted for *sarx* here "so that a sort of bridge would be established which would lead to the description of ethics as worship in the body in Rom 12."[47]

The last of the negative uses of *soma* occurs in Rom 6,6 where Paul states that as a result of baptism "we know this: our old man has been crucified so that the body of sin be rendered powerless; in order for us not to serve sin." In this passage the key to understanding lies in the use of *katargein*, which literally means "to be deprived of energy or power," and thus destroyed. Paul is saying, in much the same way as in Rom 7,24, that our potential for entering into relationships with the realm of sin has been deprived of its power because of a reality brought about in us by God's action. This takes place in and through our act of faith and the baptismal gesture, our "having become grafted into him by the likeness of his death" (Rom 6,5). The expression "body of sin" is one of the Pauline terms which occurs in the context of the new experience of life which comes with radical conversion and which is an essential component of the charismatic renewal. I would like to propose the phrase "that the body of sin be rendered powerless" to be a more extensive, but also more apt, description of what we have termed "inner healing," "healing of the memory," "healing of the heart," and "healing of relationships." Let me develop this briefly.

Paul is describing the causality of God in the act of faith he works in us, and in the baptismal gesture. Baptism is the sacrament of faith. The result is that "we are dead to sin but living for God in Christ Jesus" (Rom 6,11). The moment of baptism is a moment of confessing with one's lips that Jesus is Lord, and believing in one's heart that God raised him from the dead (see Rom 10,9; 1Cor 12,3). Paul adds, "By the heart it is believed for justification, and by the mouth it is confessed to salvation" (Rom 10,10). We should remember that "in Romans especially justification or justice is in no way made the equivalent of salvation: for justification is only the beginning of that salvation which is finally obtained with the resurrection of the body, that is, at the Parousia."[48] The tremendous power *(dynamis)* released in the personality by the inner acceptance of what God has done in Jesus Christ redounds to the profession of that faith in the essential of the Credo: Jesus is Lord. This profession made with the mouth—the corporeal personality—leads to salvation, "the redemption of our bodies" (Rom 8,23). It includes the whole process by which we offer our "bodies as a living sacrifice, holy and pleasing to God" (Rom 12,1).

There are many expressions for the act by which the Christian breaks with this age and lives a new life to God, but they are all basically linked with faith.[49] As described in Rom 6,6, the effect of faith-baptism is to render powerless for further harm that physical aspect of the human personality by which we relate to the world.

It is a common experience in the charismatic renewal to encounter people who have been baptized but who have never experienced this inefficacy of the "body of sin." They have never known in their own being what St. Thomas Aquinas describes when he says, "The act of believing is itself the first act of justice that God works in the believer, by which he believes in God as justifying, submits to his justification and thus receives its effect."[50] In other words, these people have received the sacrament but have never been evangelized.[51] When a man truly believes in his heart and confesses with his lips, he sets loose an energy, a new life, within himself. This is an ongoing process.

Accordingly, I see what we variously call inner healing, the healing of memories, etc., as a preaching of the good news. It is both word and prayer, and it helps a person yield in faith to that action of God within him by which this "body of sin" is deprived, first, of its power to create new sinful relationships; and second, of its power to use the vestiges of old associations. The bondage of those associations is most apparent in the fear and anger that they carry, and in the living knowledge of God the Father that they prevent. The "body of sin" is progressively rendered powerless by the action of faith within the personality, and the action of the Spirit in the building of faith relationships with others.

What we call "psychology," Paul would call "somatology." This gives a more sophisticated insight into the symbolic reality of man both as open to sin and death, and as the bearer of his true destiny: "If Christ is in you, the body indeed is dead because of sin, but the Spirit is life because of justification. Moreover, if the Spirit of the one who raised Jesus from the dead dwells in you, then the one who raised Christ from the dead will give life to your mortal bodies through his indwelling Spirit in you" (Rom 8,10-11).

There is one other particular instance of Pauline general usage that merits attention here for the corrective light it can throw on some notions of apostolic power. It is found in Paul's polemic against what he ironically calls "super-apostles" (2Cor 11,5; 12,11), and against the attitudes these men engendered in the Corinthian community. Certain sections of what we now have as 2 Corinthians contain various attacks against these men and a defense of Paul's apostolate.

It seems that the "super-apostles" were judaizers, probably of a gnostic or protognostic tendency, who had a great esteem for the Mosaic Law in their interpretation of it according to an "enlightened" hermeneutic of their own. They considered themselves "wise" and "spiritual," above the need to pay attention to an ethics of the body (this information is gleaned mostly from 1Cor). They were men endowed with charismatic visions and the power to perform extraordinary miracles. They presented themselves to the Corinthians bearing letters of recommendation from communities they had previously visited that could attest to the list of their wonderful accomplishments. They preached their gospel "in power" and undermined esteem for Paul by saying that he was unstable, unfaithful to his original commitment to the Mosaic Law, and "weak" in his personal presence (2Cor 10,10).[52]

Paul counters by adducing the fact that through him "the signs of an apostle were worked in your midst, in all patience [this is Paul's qualifier], with signs and wonders and works of power" (2Cor 12,12). While admitting that they have forced him to make a fool of himself (2Cor 12,11), Paul also mentions his visions and revelations (2Cor 12,1-6). He goes on in the same context, however, to speak of a "thorn for the flesh, a messenger of Satan, that he might beat me," by which he most probably means some obstacle to his apostolic efforts.[53]

This leads Paul to a discussion of the meaning of "weakness," and finally to the expression of "the fundamental law of the apostolate" (Lyonnet): "My grace is sufficient for you; for the power is brought to perfection in weakness." This word of the Lord links Paul's ministry to the mystery of the passion and resurrection of Jesus who "was crucified out of weakness, but who lives from the power of God" (2Cor 13,4). And so Paul exclaims:

> Most gladly then do I rather glory in my weaknesses so that the power of Christ may dwell over me. Therefore, I take joy in weaknesses; in insults, in hardships, in persecutions, in impossible situations for the sake of Christ; for when I am weak, that is when I am powerful. (2Cor 12,9-10)

This list of weaknesses is amplified elsewhere in a mock list of "great accomplishments" which Paul presents as a "letter of recommendation," though he insists that he needs none; the very fact that the Corinthians are believers at all is God's seal on the authenticity of his apostolate (see 2Cor 12,11; and especially 3,1-3). Paul's great deeds are deeds of "weakness"—that is, they are worked in his humanity, his body—and they are purposely chosen to provide a faith perspective on his successful and "spiritual" opponents. After carefully distinguishing the fact that he campaigns "in the flesh, but not according to the flesh" (2Cor 10,3), he sets about, somewhat later, to list his "accomplishments":

> But whatever any one dares to boast of—I am speaking as a fool—I also dare to boast of that. Are they Hebrews? So am I. Are they Israelites? So am I. Are they descendants of Abraham? So am I. Are they servants of Christ? I am a better one—I am talking like a madman—with far greater labors, far more imprisonments, with countless beatings, and often near death. Five times I have received at the hands of the Jews the forty lashes less one. Three times I have been beaten with rods; once I was stoned. Three times I have been shipwrecked; a night and a day I have been adrift at sea; on frequent journeys, in danger from rivers, danger from robbers, danger from my own people, danger from Gentiles, danger in the city, danger in the wilderness, danger at sea, danger from false brethren; in toil and hardship, through many a sleepless night, in hunger and thirst, often without food, in cold and exposure. And apart from other things, there is the daily pressure upon me of my anxiety for all the churches. Who is weak, and I am not weak? Who is made to fall, and I am not indignant? (2Cor 11, 21b-29)

All of these considerations prepare us to see the meaning of what Paul refers to in 2Cor 4,7-12 as the "dying of Jesus." I adduce this expression here because it contains another reference to *soma,* one which can purify and strengthen our experience in the charismatic renewal. I am thinking of the danger of confusing a "spiritual man"—that is, a man of the Spirit—with an imposing personality. We all run this risk, but it is especially prevalent in some charismatic groups. Although they are in no way opponents of Paul, but rather devoted friends and disciples, these groups still tend to look to powerful success in preaching, healing, and deliverance, as well as in financial and organizational ventures, as the necessary signs of true evangelism.

Paul in no way denies that signs and wonders characterize the men sent by Christ. But, as we have seen, there is a dimension of "weakness" in a deep apostolic ministry which allows the power of the resurrection to "dwell over" a person in the way that the Shekinah dwelt in the temple: as a manifestation not only of God's care, but of his presence. When we bear in mind that *soma* refers to the whole body-person as related to *life,* we see that the dying of Jesus means realizing, in one's total being, the mystery of power in weakness. By who we are, in our whole personality and life-style, we are meant to carry this treasure in such a way that Jesus is seen as the source of the power we exercise: "For what we preach is not ourselves, but Jesus Christ as Lord, and ourselves as your slaves for the sake of Jesus" (2Cor 4,5).

> But we have this treasure in earthen vessels, to show that the transcendent power belongs to God and not to us. We are afflicted in every way, but not crushed; perplexed, but not driven to despair; persecuted, but not forsaken; struck down, but not destroyed; always carrying in the body the death of Jesus, so that the life of Jesus may also be manifested in our bodies. For while we live we are always being given up to death for Jesus' sake, so that the life of Jesus may be manifested in our mortal flesh.[54] So death is at work in us, but life in you. (2Cor 4,7-12)[55]

Paul's Two Specialized Uses of Soma

We must not distinguish too sharply what we have seen thus far from the two uses we will consider briefly now. Though both of the specialized uses are creative contributions of Paul, the difference between them is not so much in kind as in extension and intensity. On the one hand, there is the meaning of *soma* as the concrete basis for glorifying God in the physical expression of one's being (see 1Cor 6,19), and on the other, that of being made "con-corporeal" with Christ and with one another (Cyril of Alexandria). Thus the two aspects of *soma* that we are going to consider now are first, its ecclesiastical dimension; and second, its sacramental dimension.[56] These two are, of course, intimately connected. We will focus more upon the first aspect because it touches more closely on what we have experienced in the charismatic renewal up to now.

1) The Church as the Body of Christ. It goes without saying that my intention here is not to resume all that has been said in recent years about this mystery. I wish merely to consider certain aspects of Pauline somatology as it is related to our present experience of the charismatic renewal. This will consist mostly in a deepening of our sense of community.

As is well known, the accent in Colossians and Ephesians is somewhat different regarding the Church as the Body of Christ than it is in 1 Corinthians and Romans.[57] It is only in the later Captivity Letters, where the term *pleroma* is used, and where there is the explicit statement, "the Church which is his Body" (Eph 1,23; see Col 1,18), that Christ is identified as the head of the Body. These are legitimate, specific developments of the original intuition, but they lie outside the scope of our investigation. In the present study, we will attempt to penetrate Paul's prophetic teaching regarding the nature of our somatic union in Christ.

The first adumbration of this teaching is found in Phil 3,21, which reads in context as follows:

> For our citizenship is in heaven, from where we are awaiting a savior, the Lord Jesus Christ, who will transform the body of our lowliness conformed to the body of his glory, according to the energy of him who is able to subject all things to him.[58]

Paul has already expressed, in blessing form, the desire that the God of peace will keep the believers for the parousia, not only in regard to their spirit, but also in their soul and in their body (1Thes 5,23; see above). In Philippians, we have the notion that there is an "energy" at work by which our body-persons will be made conformable to the body-person of the risen Christ. A more mature form of the same thought is to be found in Rom 8,10-11, as we have seen, where "energy" is replaced by "indwelling Spirit"; while in 1Cor 15,35-58, Paul grapples with the question of the kind of *soma* we will have.

We should note that from the very beginning, the link between Christ's body and ours is seen to lie in the "energy" or, in later texts, the "power" or the "Spirit" which we share. A further confirmation of this is to be found in Phil 3,8,[59] where Paul speaks of the "surpassing good of knowing my Lord Christ Jesus," and then goes on to specify: "in order to know him, and the power of his resurrection, and sharing of his sufferings, conformed to his death, if somehow I might arrive at resurrection from the dead" (Phil 3,10-11).

In 1Cor 6,12-20, a passage that ranks among the earliest sections of the Corinthian correspondence by any reckoning, we have Paul's rebuttal of the slogan, "Everything is permissible for me" (1Cor 6,12; see 1Cor 10,23)[60], and an argument against one of the consequences that the "spiritualists" drew from this slogan. Paul points out not only that the undisciplined use of the principle of indifference is not "for the best" and leads to being dominated, but also that the equation "belly for food" is not the same as "body for immorality." The belly will perish, but the body, the very physical basis of all relationships, will not; it is "for the Lord." But more than that, this union between our body and the Lord's body, this power of the resurrection which will be manifest at the eschatological moment, is operative even now:

> The body is not for immorality but for the Lord, and the Lord for the body. God raised up the Lord, and he will raise us up by his power. Do you not know that your

> bodies are the members of Christ? Will I take the members of Christ and make them members of a harlot? Never! (1Cor 6,13b-15)

The argument goes on to describe the sexual union in terms of Gn 2,24, contrasting it with becoming "one spirit" with the Lord, and then finally stating that the fornicator sins against his own body in a unique way.

The obvious conclusions we draw from this remarkable passage is that Paul is teaching that our relationship to the Lord is a corporeal one. We are being conformed to his *soma*, that is, to that physical dimension of the risen Jesus by which he is in relationship with the world and with us as body-persons. More than that, this interaction of corporeal relationship is so intimate that we make up the *soma tou Christou*, the Body of Christ.[61]

In 1Cor 12,12-31a and Rom 12,3-8, Paul is treating of the good order of the community and the proper estimation of the gifts of the Spirit. However, he does not base himself on the obvious advantages to be gained by living in a well-ordered community; rather, he has recourse to a unique principle which he expresses in various ways:

> For just as the body is one and has many members, and all the members of the body, though many, are one body, so it is with the Christ. (1Cor 12,12)[62]

> Now you are the Body of Christ and individually members of it. (1Cor 12,27)

> For as in one body we have many members, and all the members do not have the same function, so we, though many, are one body in Christ and individually members one of another. (Rom 12,4)

Many commentators have already noted[63] that there are two profound differences between Paul's application of the principles of good order in "the Body of Christ," and the common hellenistic image of the "body politic." First and foremost, Paul is always describing a concrete group of people and not merely speculating on the analogy between the human body and society. Secondly, Paul gives a name to this body; it is the body of *someone*—Christ. These differences mean that while Paul is certainly developing a common metaphor in 1Cor 12,14-24, this metaphor is a secondary application, based on the word *soma,* and not the primary source of Paul's teaching. As we have seen, his teaching has its roots in the understanding that we are one somatic reality with Christ and with one another: together in the Spirit, we form a unified whole based on our physical capacity for relationships.

What has this to say about the anthropology of the charismatic renewal? I would suggest that this teaching of Paul uncovers for us the true meaning of the move toward community. Not only is such a move a spontaneous trajectory following upon the experience of baptism, as may be seen in Acts (2,42-47; 4,32-35; 5,12-16); not only is such a banding together morally desirable for the mutual support that it can mean. There is more: a true community is a place of "mystical union" in which the totality of our personality and our spiritual, emotional, and physical life is taken up into union with these same dimensions of the risen Lord. So we live *now* "in hope" (Rom 8,24), the true meaning of man.

St. Ignatius of Antioch, describing the effect of his martyrdom, said, "When I arrive there [with the Lord] I will be a man."[64] Life in the Body of Christ is meant to begin that process right now. The most significant contribution of the charismatic renewal to Christian anthropology will lie in a deeper living of the mystery of communion in the Body of Christ, and in reflecting on that mystery in the light of the teaching of the whole corpus of Pauline writings.

2) The Sacramental Soma of Christ. The two things that

Paul tells the Corinthians he has received from tradition and passes on to them are the bodily resurrection of Christ, and the bodily presence of Christ in the Eucharist (1Cor 15,3-5; 11,23-25). I wish here to point especially to the texts concerning the Eucharist, as a prophetic call to us Catholics to bring this dimension of the apostolic heritage to full renewal for the good of all believing Christians.

Certainly, as the saints have always told us, the best preparation for understanding the Eucharist is a life in conformity with the passion and resurrection it represents. Still, it seems to me that this aspect of our somatic life in Christ is still quite unrelated to most of what we do, plan, and realize in faith in the charismatic renewal. Our unity in Christ will never arrive at its true body-person intensity without a yielding of our beings to that movement of the Holy Spirit which renders the flesh of Christ *vivificatam et vivificantem*.[65] The Eucharist is the Body of Christ; it is the person of the Lord in his transformed physical reality, joined "in one Spirit" to all who cling to him (see 1Cor 6,17).

Paul speaks in 1Cor 10,16-17 of the sharing (the same word as the "sharing" of the sufferings of Christ in Phil 3,10) in the blood and the *soma* of Christ. The act by which we enter into a committed relationship with the Lord and with one another, and break bread in his memory, becomes the physical, dynamic means by which Christ makes us one in our whole human reality:

> The cup of blessing which we bless, is it not a sharing in the blood of Christ? The bread which we break, is it not a sharing in the body of Christ? Because there is one bread, we the many *are one body* for we all partake of the one bread. (1Cor 10,16-17, emphasis supplied)

In 1Cor 11,17ff, Paul lists three sins against the Body: (a) "there are divisions among you"; (b) "it is not the Lord's supper you eat; for each one takes his own meal"; (c) "you despise the Church of God and humiliate those who have nothing." In correcting these abuses, Paul begins with the tradition of the Lord's self-giving, and the physical reality of that gift: "This is my body which is for you."

This is the basis of our life in Christ. It is the celebration of this memory of the Lord, as one body—not torn by divisions, not self-seeking, not making light of the poor—that is the proclamation of the death of the Lord until he comes. Our failure in this regard means that "many of you are weak and ill, and some have fallen asleep." For not only are we sent to preach the gospel and "heal every disease and infirmity" (Mt 10,1), but we are also meant to "discern the Body," to realize the physical presence of the Lord among us in his gift of the "one bread" and in our brethren, and to provide what men call "a healthy atmosphere" worthy of human life.

The Lord wants the renewal to mature and become as realistic as he is. What he has begun will reach its fruition if we show forth once again in our bodies, our whole personalities, that we are "one body in Christ." But we have courage, for in some dim way we do discern the Body, and experience in ourselves the loving power of the Lord. We know, as St. Ephrem has told us, that "he who eats this bread with faith, at the same time eats the fire of the Holy Spirit."[66] We know too that the Lord is at work even now, transforming "the body of our lowliness, conformed to the body of his glory" (Phil 3,20). As we enter into the mystery of the Eucharist, we will truly become "one body, one spirit in Christ."

NOTES

1. The remarks of those assigned to respond to this paper were most valuable, and one of them has been included in this published version. However, to have included them all would have been to deprive the responses of much of their meaning. In addition, it should be remarked that a study such as this can only be a pioneer effort. I hope in the near future to do an in-depth analysis of hermeneutics and experience, linking more closely the insights of Bernard Lonergan and Juan Luis Segundo, and developing the notion of experience being elaborated by Heribert Mühlen and others in the charismatic renewal.
2. For a good study of the present state of hermeneutics, see the following: R. E. Palmer, *Hermeneutics, Interpretation Theory in Schleiermacher, Dilthey, Heidegger and Gadamer,* Northwestern University Studies in Phenomenology and Existential Philosophy (Evanston: Northwestern University, 1969); J. M. Robinson, J.B. Cobb, eds., *The New Hermeneutic* (New York: Harper and Row, 1964). An application of some of this to theology can be found in R. Ommen, "The Hermeneutic of Dogma," *Theological Studies,* Vol. 35(1974), pp. 605-631.
3. W. Wink, *The Bible in Human Transformation* (Philadelphia: Fortress, 1973).
4. P. Dreyfus, "Exégèse en Sorbonne, exégèse en Eglise," *Revue biblique,* 82, Vol. 3(July 1975), pp. 321-359.
5. F. Herzog, "Liberation Hermeneutic as Ideology Critique?" *Interpretation,* Vol. 28 (1974), pp. 387-403.
6. T. Kuhn, "The Structure of Scientific Revolutions," 2nd ed., *International Encyclopedia of Unified Sciences,* 2,2 (Chicago: Chicago University, 1970), p. 92.
7. See the study by M. Masterman, "The Nature of a Paradigm" in I. Lakatos, E. Musgrave, eds., *Criticism and the Growth of Knowledge* (Cambridge: Cambridge University Press, 1970), pp. 59-89.
8. For a brief discussion of the view of exegesis and hermeneutics, see D. Patte, *What is Structural Exegesis?* (Philadelphia: For-

tress, 1976). For a slightly different view, see the remarks in note 11.
9. See once again the work by Palmer, *Hermeneutics;* see also the article on hermeneutics by K. Lehmann in *Sacramentum Mundi,* Vol. 3(New York: Herder and Herder, 1968), pp. 23-27.
10. Quoted by I. Barbour, *Myths, Models and Paradigms, the Nature of Scientific and Religious Language* (London: S.C.M. Press, 1974), p. 95.
11. In this sense, it is more exact to speak of exegesis as the science of interpretation, as a disciplined effort to share in what is communicated by a text. Hermeneutics is the epistemology of communication.
12. Without some continuity, there can be no intelligibility. The rupture in "tradition" offered by prophetic interpretation of that tradition comes about because the principle of continuity has become the principle of conformity. In this sense all narrow conservatism is, at its root, a lack of faith.
13. It is worth quoting here some lines of Palmer, *Hermeneutics,* p. 14:

> Yet one may note that the fundamental 'Hermes process' is at work: . . . something foreign, strange, separated in time, space, or experience is made familiar, present, comprehensible; something requiring representation, explanation, or translation is somehow 'brought to understanding'—is 'interpreted.'

14. J.L. Segundo, *The Liberation of Theology* (New York: Orbis, 1976), p. 9. There are other, less universally applicable aspects of liberation theology that do not enter into our discussion here. One aspect that particularly calls for close modification is, in my opinion, the insistence on the necessity of the dialectic of conflict.
15. The phrase is, of course, Abraham Heschel's. For a slightly different application of this principle, see F. Martin, "In Justice," *Touching God* (New York: Dimension, 1975), ch. 14.
16. Vatican Council II, *Decree on Revelation,* par. 12. For a study of this phrase, see D. Barsotti, *La parola e lo spirito* (Milano: Edizioni O.R., 1971).
17. *Segundo,* op.cit., pp. 25ff.

18. *Ibid.*, p. 10. The italics are in the text of the English translation.
19. It should be noted here that Cone's article, "Biblical Revelation and Social Existence," *Interpretation,* Vol. 28(1974), pp. 422-440, comes much closer to being a true biblical hermeneutics.
20. Another way of envisaging the hermeneutic circle was traced out by Bernard Lonergan in his description of conversion as the foundation for theological methodology. He sketches it out in the following words:

> . . . conversion occurs in the lives of individuals. It is not merely a change or even a development; rather it is a radical transformation on which follows, on all levels of living, an interlocked series of changes and developments. What hitherto was unnoticed becomes vivid and present. What had been of no concern becomes a matter of high import . . . In a current expression, conversion is ontic. The convert apprehends differently, values differently, relates differently, because he has become different . . . Though conversion is intensely personal, utterly intimate, still it is not so private as to be solitary. It can happen to many and they can form a community to sustain one another in their self-transformation and to help one another in working out the implications, and in fulfilling the promise of their new life . . . It follows that reflection on conversion can supply theology with its foundation and, indeed, with a foundation that is concrete, dynamic, personal, communal, and historical.

This quotation is drawn from Lonergan's article, "Theology in its New Context," in L.K. Shook, ed., *Theology of Renewal,* Proceedings of the Congress on the Theology of the Renewal of the Church, Centenary of Canada, 1967 (Montreal: Palm, 1968), pp. 34-47; quote is from pp. 44-45. See also Lonergan's remarks in *Method in Theology* (New York: Herder and Herder, 1972), especially Ch. 11, "Foundations."
21. W. Pannenberg, *What is Man?* (Philadelphia: Fortress, 1970), reference to M. Scheler, p. 3, n. 1; J. Moltmann, *Man* (Philadelphia: Fortress, 1974), reference to Scheler and Herder, pp. 5ff.

22. W. Pannenberg, *op.cit.*, p. 6.
23. See especially, *One Dimensional Man* (Boston: Beacon, 1964); *Eros and Civilization* (Boston: Beacon, 1955).
24. See especially, *Being and Having* (London: Collins, 1965).
25. See especially, *The Technological Society* (New York: Knopf, 1964).
26. R. Coe, *Sociology of Medicine* (New York: McGraw-Hill, 1970), p. 98. See also T. Parsons, *The Social System* (Glencoe, Illinois: Free Press, 1951). For much of the information in this section, I am indebted to unpublished work by Professor Bruce Malina and other members of the Task Force on "Healing in the New Testament," who meet regularly as part of the annual sessions of the Catholic Biblical Association of America.
27. *Yale Journal of Biology and Medicine,* Vol. 43(1971), pp. 385-407; quote is from p. 402. For an application of these principles, though one that needs modification, see R.C. Finacune, "The Use and Abuse of Medieval Miracles," *History,* Vol. 60(1975), pp. 1-10.
28. See, for instance, C. Talavera, "The Charismatic Renewal and Christian Social Commitment in Latin America," Part I, *New Covenant,* 6,2(August 1976), pp. 4-8; Part II, *New Covenant,* 6,3(September 1976), pp. 12-16.
29. *Forms of Symbolic Action,* Proceedings of the 1969 Annual Spring Meeting of the American Ethnological Society (Seattle: University of Washington, no date), pp. 69-80; quote is from p. 71. Ms. Douglas also makes the following interesting observation:

> . . . since university life itself is a form of withdrawal from society, university teachers will be more inclined to dichotomize spirit and flesh than other professions more centrally involved in administration, business and government, and this tendency would influence their research and teaching. (p. 70).

30. Jörg Splett, "Body," *Sacramentum Mundi,* Vol. 16 (New York: Herder and Herder, 1968), p. 235; cf. also K. Rahner, "The Corporeal Nature of Freedom and its Sphere," *Grace and Freedom* (New York: Herder, 1969), pp. 232-235.
31. *De Resurrectione Carnis,* 8,2. For an excellent study of this

aspect of man in the Christian life, see C. Vagaggini, *The Flesh, Instrument of Salvation*, (New York: Alba, 1968).
32. Vatican Council II, *Pastoral Constitution on the Church in the Modern World*, opening line.
33. H. Mouroux, *The Christian Experience* (New York: Sheed and Ward, 1954), p. 15; see also H. Mühlen's article and book.
34. I am thinking here of the analyses of "rapture," "ecstasy," etc., undertaken in the works considered classical during the last twenty years or so: those by Garrigou-Lagrange, Lehodey, Poulain, etc. For a more extended treatment of some aspects of the same preoccupation, see H. Thurston, *The Physical Phenomena of Mysticism* (London: Burns Oates, 1951).
35. *Commentary on John* 11, 11; *P.G.* 74, pp. 557ff. Quoted in Vagaggini, *op. cit.*, p. 93.
36. Among the many studies that could be referred to here, the following may be mentioned: H.W. Wolff, *Anthropology of the Old Testament* (Philadelphia: Fortress, 1974); W. Eichrodt, *Man in the Old Testament*, Studies in Biblical Theology, ser. 1, no. 4 (London: S.C.M., 1951); A. Gelin, *The Concept of Man in the Bible* (New York: Alba, 1967); W. Mork, *The Biblical Meaning of Man* (Milwaukee: Bruce, 1967).
37. *Arbeiten zur Geschichte des antiken Judentums und Urchristentums*, 10 (Leiden: Brill, 1971).
38. Published by the Cambridge University Press, 1976.
39. Jewett's study tends to seek an explanation for all of Paul's terminological usage in the fact that he is responding to opponents (as the subtitle of his work indicates), while Gundry, engaged as he is in a polemic against the Bultmann-Robinson contention that "*soma* equals personality" seems unaware that his own concept of "body" derives from a particular twentieth century "objective" notion.
40. Jewett, "The History of Research," *Paul's Anthropological Terminology*, pp. 201-250.
41. We will not need to enter here into the complex question regarding the number and chronology of the portions of letters that make up the Corinthian correspondence. Also, we will treat Philippians as a single letter.
42. For a bibliography on this and other points, I refer the reader to the studies of Jewett and Gundry. In regard to the background of

soma, special mention should be made of the study of Schweizer in the *Theological Dictionary of the New Testament,* Vol. 7, pp. 1024-1094. We should also mention the very influential work of J.A.T. Robinson, *The Body, Studies in Biblical Theology,* ser. 1, 5 (London: S.C.M., 1957).

43. Jewett is correct in maintaining that Paul does not follow his fellow rabbis and other New Testament authors in interchanging *psyche* and *pneuma,* as he does in these cases with *soma* and *sarx*.
44. For an ample discussion of this verse, see B. Rigaux, "Les épîtres aux thessaloniciens," *Etudes bibliques* (Paris: Gabalda, 1956), pp. 596-600.
45. See: S. Lyonnet, *Exegesis Epistulae ad Romanos,* Chs. 5-8. (Rome: privately published at the Pontifical Biblical Institute, 1961), pp. 104ff.
46. Jewett, *Paul's Anthropological Terminology,* p. 67.
47. *Ibid.,* p. 290. Jewett is applying this explanation to all three instances of *soma* which we have been considering; for Rom 12, see E. Käseman, "Worship in Everyday Life," *New Testament Questions of Today* (London: S.C.M., 1969), pp. 168-182.
48. S. Lyonnet, *Quaestiones in Epistulam ad Romanos,* Series Altera (Rome: privately published at the Pontifical Biblical Institute, 1975), p. 92.
49. See J. Hamer, "Le baptême et la foi," *Irenikon,* (1950), pp. 387-405.
50. St. Thomas on Rom 4, 5.
51. We may legitimately wonder how many have received the fullness of the sacrament. St. Thomas, commenting on Gal 3, 27, writes, "Baptism does not come about [fit] except in faith without which we would in no way attain the effect of baptism."
52. This reconstruction of Paul's opponents owes much to the close study by D. Georgi, *Die Gegner des Paulus im 2 Korintherbrief, Studien zur religiösen Propaganda in der Spätantike* (Neukirchen: 1964). However, Georgi's reliance on the category of "divine man" seems to me to be chronologically misplaced.
53. See. S. Lyonnet, "The Fundamental Law of the Apostolate as Formulated and Lived by St. Paul (2Cor 12,9)" in I. de la Potterie, S. Lyonnet, *The Christian Lives by the Spirit* (New York: Alba, 1971), pp. 245-266.

54. As was mentioned previously, this usage here of *sarx* is at least neutral, and is one of those places in which Paul interchanges *soma* and *sarx*.
55. For another description of preaching the gospel as a "priestly service," see Rom 15, 15-20.
56. Thus, among other important Pauline usages not considered here, there is especially the question of the eschatological destiny of the *soma* as this is treated in 1Cor 15, 1-58; and the difficult but important 2Cor 5,1-10. On this latter text, see F.G. Lang, "2. Korinther 5,1-10 in der neueren Forschung," *Beiträge zur Geschichte der biblischen Exegesis,* 16 (Tübingen: Mohr, 1973).
57. See P. Benoit, "Corps, tête, et plérôme dans les épîtres de la Captivité," *Exégèse et théologie,* t. 2 (Paris: Cerf, 1961), pp. 107-153.
58. It is possible to read this text in a slightly different way by replacing the possessive pronoun; thus, "who will transform our body of lowliness, conformed to his body of glory."
59. For a good summary of present thinking on the composition and destination of Philippians, see F.W. Beare, "The Epistle to the Philippians," *Black's New Testament Commentaries* (London: Black, 1973), pp. 4ff.
60. For a discussion of this, see H. Conzelmann, *1 Corinthians,* Hermeneia (Philadephia: Fortress, 1975), pp. 109ff.
61. Jewett's words, as he concludes his study of 1Cor 6, 12-20, are worth quoting here:

> My conclusion is that *soma* as the basis of corporal relationship is the chosen seat of the divine spirit. To be physically joined with Christ means to be one spirit with him and neither goes without the other. It follows that one's body does not belong to himself alone but to Christ who bought it for himself (1Cor. 6:19b-20a), and that therefore it is appropriate to glorify God through the body (1 Cor. 6:20b).

62. For the phrase "The Christ," see 1Cor 1,13.
63. See, for example: L. Cerfaux, "La théologie de l'Eglise suivant saint Paul," 3me ed., *Unam Sanctam,* 54 (Paris: Cerf, 1965), pp. 224ff.
64. "Letter to the Romans," 6,1-7,3; *Sources chrétiennes* 10, pp. 132-136.

65. Vatican Council II, *Decree on the Ministry and Life of Priests*, par. 5.
66. Quoted by P. Evdokimov in *l'Esprit-Saint dans la tradition orthodoxe* (Paris: 1969), p. 98.

A RESPONSE TO FRANCIS MARTIN'S PAPER
Carroll Stuhlmueller, C.P.

Fr. Martin explores two topics that lie at the center of all biblical study. The initial discussion focuses upon *hermeneutical rules* or correct methodology, assuring people, so far as is humanly possible, that their scriptural interpretation follows the intentions of the Holy Spirit. The second half of Fr. Martin's essay investigates *biblical anthropology* or the human arena where God intervened to redeem his people, to sustain the memory of these wondrous interventions, and eventually to transfer the oral traditions into a library of sacred books.

In both hermeneutics and anthropology, Fr. Martin insists that one follow a "principle of continuity" within the long span of time throughout the Old Testament into the New. "A faith experience," moreover, must assure "a genuine coalescence of horizons between the authors of the NT, and those who receive their message today."

My own observations are set in motion by the presence of evolutionary leaps within the continuity of the Bible. These explosive moments usually took Israel or the disciples of Jesus by surprise. Yet, on later reflection, they were seen to have preexisted in a long gestation period and so never to have broken the continuity. Hermeneutics, accordingly, must allow for the element of "surprise" within its rules of biblical interpretation. Not only do the *mirabilia Dei* or wondrous acts of divine intervention form a substantive element in the history of salvation, but hermeneutics by its rules and suggestions must dispose the reader to reexperience the wonders. Here the charismatic renewal finds its proper role.

In the Bible the classic formulas of faith link together God's wondrous deeds in the establishment and ongoing history of Israel and the Church. The Ten Commandments begin with Israel's confesson of the divine word: "I, the Lord, am your God, who brought you out of the land of Egypt, that place of slavery" (Ex 20,2; Dt 5,6). This line by itself is considered so important by the Jewish people, that they call it their first commandment. More extensive credal formulas occur in Dt 26,5-10 and Jos 24. Deuteronomy expresses Israel's awe at God's great redemptive acts:

> Ask now of the days of old, before your time, ever since God created man upon the earth; ask from one end of the sky to the other: Did anything so great ever happen before? . . . Or did any god venture to go and take a nation for himself from the midst of another nation, by testings, by signs and wonders, by war, with his strong hand and outstretched arm, and by great terrors, all of which the Lord, your God, did for you in Egypt before your very eyes. (Dt 4,32,34)

Miracles such as these were not a common occurrence. In fact, that same chapter of Deuteronomy insists upon normal human responses such as obeying the divine "statutes and commandments" and teaching them to one's children (Dt 4,40). Nonetheless, within the continuity of human existence, history was catapulted forward at certain pivotal moments by signs and wonders.

The classic "creeds" of Israel and the Church are not so much statements of major doctrines as they are a record of God's marvelous deeds within biblical history and anthropology. Miracles occupy an integral part within the message of salvation. For this message to be interpreted correctly, biblical hermeneutics must accept miracles in the Bible, and through the Bible in life today. These points were made con-

RESPONSE

vincingly by Alfons Weiser in the booklet, *The Miracles of Jesus Then and Now* (Franciscan Herald Press, 1434 W. 51st St., Chicago 60609), who refers to such passages as Mt 11,21-22, Lk 11,14-23 and 2Cor 12,12.

Miracles, then, are an integral part of biblical history and its message of salvation; they must also be expected within the interpretation and living of the Bible today. When prophecy reaches fulfillment within our daily existence, an element of surprise should be present. Such anyway is the conviction of the prophet called Second or Deutero-Isaiah (author of Is 40-55) in a series of poems about "First and Last" (Is 41,21-29; 42,8-9; 43,8-13; etc.).

In 48,3 Second Isaiah summarizes his conclusions:

> Things of the past I foretold long ago,
>> they went forth from my mouth, I let you hear of them;
>
> then suddenly I took action and they came to be.

The key word here is "suddenly." The Hebrew form, *pith`om,* always strikes a note of surprise, as in Mal 3,1:

> Lo, I am sending my messenger
>> to prepare the way before me;
>
> And suddenly there will come to the temple
>> the Lord whom you seek,
>
> And the messenger of the covenant whom you desire.

Wonder and surprise ought to characterize the messenger of the gospel.

Biblical prophecy, therefore, does far more than announce the details of the future. If that were the case, we could quote the Bible to God and thereby force God to act within its clear words and our obvious understanding of them! While prophecy maintains a strong line of continuity from biblical events and books into our own contemporary anthropology, it also prepares us to await the wonder, the surprise, the overwhelmingly explosive action of God within the continuity.

When Fr. Martin drew the attention of the charismatic renewal to biblical hermeneutics and anthropology, he enabled us to draw up some good guidelines: (1) biblical anthropology presumes divine intervention within human existence; (2) hermeneutics attributes an integral place to miracles within the message of salvation; (3) the fulfillment of prophecy will always include the element of surpise. These miracles are not necessarily plastic copies of the biblical ones. Fundamentalism, therefore, turns out to be bad hermeneutics. Miracles prepare for miracles. Charismatic renewal envigorates such faith.

NEW ASPECTS OF SPIRITUAL DIRECTION
Ernest E. Larkin, O.Carm.

The object of this paper is to examine certain practices of spiritual direction in the Catholic charismatic renewal in the light of the history of spiritual direction in the Church. The paper will be tentative because practices in the renewal are not uniform, and the tradition of spiritual direction is both rich and protean.[1]

The very concept of spiritual direction varies with authors so that contradictory affirmations abound on the subject. Frequently, for example, it is said that the role of the director is to make himself superfluous, to train his client to be self-directing. Yet St. Bernard writes, "He who makes himself his own director becomes the disciple of a fool."[2] An Italian Salesian, E. Valentini, writing in 1950, asserts that spiritual direction is necessary for most religious because they remain in the purgative way.[3] James Walsh, S.J. agrees with the premise that most religious are beginners, but he draws an opposite conclusion, namely, that they do not need spiritual direction; spiritual direction presupposes a "special call," a "gripping drive" and "ache" for divine union, an advanced disposition far down the road.[4]

If "direction" means psychological counseling or educational guidance, then surely the director has a temporary role, and his primary thrust will be the novices in the spiritual life. James Walsh and perhaps St. Bernard have something else in mind.

Kinds of Spiritual Direction

Any helping relationship that has the spiritual development of a person as the consciously willed object can be called spiritual direction. I would attempt to clarify the meaning of the term by distinguishing between general and special spiritual direction.

General spiritual direction is an introduction into the life in the Spirit. It sets the stage and secures the necessary conditions for spiritual growth. It thus includes education and formation, pastoring and spiritual government; as well as guidance and counseling insofar as these are informational and psychological functions respectively.

Special spiritual direction is more personalized, more grace-oriented, more explicitly spiritual. It deals directly with the individual, and precisely with that person's relationship with God. Its focus is the particular will of God: how this individual is being moved and touched by God. The general relationships look to the human conditions; spiritual direction as such tunes into the God-dimension, uncovering, identifying, and helping the person to appropriate the action of God in his soul. It is best understood as the correlative of the manifestation of conscience, and without such manifestation it does not exist.

"Manifestation of conscience" needs clarification. It is self-revelation, not so much in terms of sins or virtues or deliberate acts, but as an accounting of the impulses, ideas, attractions, and repulsions that precede judgment or deliberation. It is the necessary input for discernment of spirits. Schaefer describes manifestation of conscience as the revelation of one's "state of soul, outside of confession, namely of those matters which are proximately connected with virtues and vices. It is the revealing of one's *mores,* affections, inclinations, propensities, temptations, dangers and passions."[5] The restriction, "outside of confession," serves to distinguish confessional matters, which are deliberate sins, from non-deliberate interior movements, which may be from God or the evil spirit and which are properly the terrain of the spiritual director as such.[6]

This paper is concerned with both general and special direction. For purposes of clarity, however, I will use the term "spiritual direction" only in the special sense.

General Spiritual Direction

General spiritual direction can be summed up in three forms: guidance, government, and counseling. It may be helpful to identify each form more clearly.

Guidance. Guidance is basically, though not exclusively, intellectual. The spiritual guide teaches the truth with every instrumentality available: good example, a loving, "enabling" relationship, communication, and teaching techniques. A truer designation would be "education," whether moral or spiritual, or "formation," either initial or continuing. "Spiritual guidance" is the term more frequently found in the literature, though not always in the precise sense used here.

Whatever the term, the function is clear: Spiritual guidance, education, or formation is the process that has in view changes in behavioral patterns, attitudes, value systems, and ways of thinking and acting. A living community or fellowship is rightly considered to be the chief agent of this change,[7] but a "director" or educator guides the process. In one formulation, formation is described as "a process involving four major variables common to all instructional settings: learner, subject matter, environment, and teacher. A formation director is a teacher who orchestrates the four variables to produce specific outcomes."[8]

Government. Guidance is closely aligned to spiritual government, or what charismatics call pastoral direction or "shepherding" (Eph 4,11).[9] The superior of a religious community, the pastor of a parish, and the leader of a prayer group give pastoral direction to their particular groupings. Their exercise of authority or leadership in their communities ultimately has in view the spiritual advancement of each member. The role coincides with teaching insofar as the leader promotes good discipline, morality, and spiritual living by speaking "to men for their upbuilding, their encouragement, their consolation . . . [and] upbuilding of the church" (1Cor 14,3,5).

But the pastor is more than a teacher; he looks to all the spiritual needs of the group. In developing the role of pastor or shepherd, scripture draws upon the rich background of Israel's nomadic and agrarian experience, delineating the care and concern, the loving commitment even to the laying down of one's life, the patience, courage, wisdom, and inventiveness that mark the good shepherd.

Some institutionalized forms of pastoral direction are more closely identified with guidance or formation than with leadership as such. There are, for example, the roles of novice master or seminary spiritual director. They illustrate the "institutionalized" model of spiritual direction, having as their chief function the handing on of an objective spirituality appropriate for those being initiated or renewed in a certain life style.[10] Such indoctrination must leave room for personal response and personalized growth, but this factor is secondary to the foundational work of attitudinal and value changes.

Beginners are generally better served by learning to integrate and internalize objective norms and patterns. They are not as yet spiritually mature, nor are they at that point of profound openness to God's will that John of the Cross calls detachment, Ignatius Loyola names indifference, and Hans Urs von Balthasar identifies as biblical faith.[11] This spiritual maturity is the prerequisite for the delicate discernment of God's particular concrete will. All that Ignatius proposed for beginners was "some instruction and attainment of a certain peace of soul."[12] The achievement of that peace of soul has found an effective instrument in the modern discipline of psychological counseling, the third and final form of general spiritual direction.

Counseling. Psychological counseling helps an individual sort out his feelings and recognize conflicts, and make decisions toward their resolution. The core of a therapeutic counseling relationship is a healthy interpersonal relationship, or more specifically, a set of positive attitudes of understanding, acceptance, insight, and communication. Even in its technically "directive" forms it is nondirective. The relationship itself is the source of therapy, and for this reason (among others) a great deal of good counseling occurs in informal settings among friends or between a respected significant other and one's self. The same good effects occur in group interaction.

Psychological counseling applied to religious areas is called pastoral counseling. It is the most popular of the spiritual helping relationships today. In the minds of some, pastoral counseling has replaced spiritual direction either in its form of group process[13] or in a modified form of a one-to-one counseling relationship.[14] No doubt the dynamics of counseling can contribute a great deal to good spiritual direction, but they will not replace it. The source of healing and growth in spiritual direction is the power of God mediated through the directive functioning of his minister. Henri Nouwen catches the uniqueness of the skilled counselor who is at the same time an experienced spiritual director when he describes the abbot of the Abbey of the Genesee:

> Father John Eudes Bamberger . . . listened to me with care and interest, but also with a deep conviction and a clear vision; he gave me much time and attention but did not allow me to waste a minute; he left me fully free to express my feelings and thoughts but did not hesitate to present his own; he offered me space to deliberate about

choices and to make decisions but did not withhold his opinion that some choices and decisions were better than others; he let me find my own way but did not hide the map that showed the right direction. In our conversation, John Eudes emerged not only as a listener but also as a guide, not only as a counselor but also as a director.[15]

Special Spiritual Direction

Spiritual direction in the strict sense is partly a derivative and partly an addition to the three functions considered thus far. It participates in all three, and has often been identified with one or other of them, but is reducible to none of these categories. At various times in history the spiritual director was an educator or a superior, and today as often as not he is a counselor. In the beginning, for example, among hermits of the desert such as Anthony, the spiritual father was a teacher who eventually liberated his charge and sent him off to live his own solitary life as a monk. With Pachomian cenobitism and the development of monasticism in the Middle Ages, the spiritual director became the superior, the abbot of the monastery. In both cases, however, he was a "father," a transmitter of life, and not a mere instructor or enforcer of rules and practices.

Superior and spiritual director were united in the one office during the middle years of the Church, and there was then no distinction in practice between the internal and external forum. The two forums were separated by the Irish monks in the seventh century when they connected spiritual direction with confession. In the ages of casuistry, when rules of thumb and moral systems of probabilism replaced the exercise of the virtue of prudence, the "director of conscience" exercised an almost unilateral power as the exponent of God's will and the decision maker for his penitent. This style of spiritual direction predominated in the recent past and has given spiritual direction a questionable reputation. Many of our contemporaries tend to think of spiritual direction as arbitrary, manipulative, moralistic, and imperialistic.

The Ideal Role of the Spiritual Director. A spiritual director helps a person to understand his spiritual state, to discern which decisions are appropriate to make, and to distinguish authentic movements of the Spirit from impulses that are counterfeit. His central task, therefore, is in the area of discernment of spirits.

To perform the task of confirming the direction of the Spirit in his client's life, certain preliminaries are necessary. Friedrich Wulf indicates these preliminaries when he lists the objectives for the client: 1) self-knowledge; 2) self-acceptance; 3) detachment from self; 4) specifically recognizing and accepting God's will.[16]

In this process the director is a teacher and a counselor; he also exercises an authority of recognized competence. He receives not obedience, since he is not a superior, but docility and submission from his client.[17] This concept of spiritual direction tends to consign the direction of beginners to general direction. The more advanced the client, the more there is room for special spiritual direction.

The spiritual director in the Christian tradition is another John the Baptizer, a friend of the Bridegroom and friend to the client, who points out the one Teacher who is the way, the truth, and the life. He is mentor as well as friend, not a mere occasional consultant, but a confidant who shares the other's life on a regular basis. He is the delegate and voice of the Christian community, who objectifies, clarifies, and evaluates the inner experience of the action of the Spirit in the personal life of the client, and approves and confirms the inner truth of this action as well. He is not necessarily a superior, not need he have an office in the institutional Church. But he should exercise his charismatic office in collaboration with hierarchical authority. This relationship to the official Church has led commentators in the past to urge lay people who exercise a ministry of spiritual direction to submit their ministry on a regular basis to a priest, who serves as a representative of the total Church. In this way he leaves the final judgment, the last word, to ecclesiastical authority.

Qualifications of the Spiritual Director. Today, as through the centuries, the spiritual director is a spiritual father who communicates the life of Christ as he has experienced it in his own personal life. For this reason, personal experience of the way to the Father is the first requisite of a spiritual director. Knowledge, whether spiritual, theological, psychological, or methodological, takes second place among the qualifications. Contrary to popular belief, this is true even in the mind of St. Teresa of Avila, at least in her major texts.[18] Direction, therefore, is less an action than a human relationship animated by the Spirit of God.

A person submits to an experienced man of God, not as to one who will make decisions for him, but as to one who enables him to see clearly and choose wisely. The two parties to the dialogue share their life in the Spirit in a two-way communication that has as its goal God's word for the client in the here and now. Full responsibility for decisions taken remains with the client. Practitioners of spiritual direction believe that the Lord himself uses this faith relationship to allow his word to be heard and his direction followed. The Father speaks through the spiritual father, the true Shepherd calls his sheep by name through human voices that are his instrument, and the real director of souls is the Spirit himself. It is obvious that no mere mechanical medium, such as books or tapes or even computers, will ever be able to replace the living relationship that is spiritual direction.

One final question remains: Is a group able to fulfill the function of spiritual direction? Some have developed models of formal direction in which the whole group, particularly a peer group, searches out together the will of the Father.[19]

Others describe the informal give-and-take of everyday life as one way of direction.[20] This second type is exemplified by the human interaction that goes on in groups or among friends bent on the same goal.

Both formal and informal group direction are like spiritual friendships. They are humanistic forms of spiritual direction very suitable to our anthropocentric times. No doubt the major part of the spiritual direction taking place in the world is of this variety. But in my opinion, neither formal group direction nor the informal interaction of good community life gets beyond the boundaries of general spiritual direction. It is a beginning, a help toward establishing personal norms and a spiritual discipline, but it fails to draw out the implications and unpack the deep encounter of God that mystically reveals God's special leading.

Spiritual Direction in the Catholic Charismatic Renewal

The Catholic charismatic renewal is both continuous and discontinuous with traditional spirituality. As a spiritual revival it is experiencing new leadings of the Spirit. The effects are the recovery of old truths and the evolution of new forms of Christian life.

The ongoing action of the Spirit, and the interdependence of the members of the Body of Christ are two central principles in the renewal. A spirituality organized around these two principles will give crucial importance to discernment, in order that self-deception and illuminism be avoided. It will also offer a new appreciation of mutual submission (Phil 2,3-4), and it will highlight the complementarity of the charisms (1Cor 12, 27) and the corporate nature of the Christian enterprise. These factors have led to a rebirth of interest in general and special spiritual direction and have affected the forms that this direction is taking.

Spiritual formation, pastoral care, individual counseling, and spiritual direction are thriving in the renewal. Instruction and counseling abound.[21] The mammoth book and tape ministries, teaching conferences and sharing sessions of many varieties, endless hours of "talking through" problems or praying for healing in families, in households, or over the telephone are witnesses to this fact. Leaders take their shepherding role seriously, searching scripture to understand the meaning of pastoral care and spending long hours each week in core meetings and individual counseling.

Structures to handle all this interaction have been developing as needs are recognized. Charismatics are as innocent as are others of the formal distinctions drawn in the first part of this paper. The difference, however, is that all these functions for personal and community growth are key concerns and major involvements for them. They rush to the task without a great deal of understanding about how teaching, ruling, counseling, and spiritual direction are best carried out. Nor are they concerned about the interrelationships of these ministries or their specific differences. They proceed, trusting in the leading of the Spirit and the goodwill of their brothers and sisters more than in the checks and balances of a well-coordinated religious regimen such as has evolved over the centuries in religious life. Structures like strong leadership, headship, life in the Spirit and foundation seminars, core groups, and prayer rooms have emerged to teach, guide, and direct. Our purpose here is to look at this kind of activity in the light of history and the systematic considerations developed in the first part of this paper.

Lay Directed

One obvious aspect of the general and special spiritual direction ministries in the charismatic renewal is their lay character. The Catholic charismatic renewal has broken out of the clerical mold. It does not look to priests or religious as such for direction, but to persons with charismatic experience. If these be priests or religious, or trained in theology or counseling, so much the better. But the real qualification for a service role is experience.

This is perfectly in accord with tradition. "Experience" in this context does not mean "experiences," but rather the total effect of conversion on all levels of the personality with the consequent spiritual maturity of an "adept." "No one gives what he doesn't have" is as true in spiritual matters as in material ones. By its very nature, this Christian maturity includes a certain understanding of life in Christ. Often, however, this knowledge is not objectified, reflected on, or evaluated. It is subject to all the vagaries of subjectivity without the control of the community experience past and present. It is not integrated into the tradition.

Failure to undertake this theological reflection indicates a defect in the requisite knowledge of the spiritual life, the second qualification for direction. Without such knowledge, teaching and formation are impossible, and spiritual government and counseling are severely handicapped. The quality of prudence which must guide the relationships is hardly possible without a knowledge that goes beyond the confines of one's individual experience. All three qualities—experience, knowledge, and prudence—are necessary for engaging in direction. An imprudent administrator or an ignorant teacher or a disturbed counselor does more harm than good, even if he claims to have a call from God to perform these tasks. The lack of qualification proves that there is no such call.

This does not mean that only persons with degrees in theology or a long in-service apprenticeship are equipped to teach, lead, counsel, or direct. It does, however, mean that spiritual directors must get the training and preparation somewhere. The Lord gives charisms where he wills and he chooses the weak things of this world to confound the strong (1Cor 1,27). But good fruits are necessary validations for the presence of a charism. These will be absent if incompetent persons are attempting the work. Charisms function in concrete persons, not in a vacuum. If a person is unable to carry out the task, he does not have the charism. A charism may well supply for the lack of natural qualities in an extraordinary case; it is only prudent, however, to expect educated persons to be recipients of a teaching charism, emotionally balanced persons to be selected for counseling, and holy persons to be spiritual directors.

Unqualified persons should be dissuaded from giving direction. Overseeing is important here, and guidelines, perhaps from the National Service Committee or from the Bishops' Ad Hoc Committee, are long overdue to help prayer groups and communities identify those persons who are candidates for directive roles.[22] The question here is knowledge and prudence, not any particular form of training. Training in the religious disciplines, however, is not to be disdained; and one wonders why older, established charismatic communities do not seem to be thinking of sending their future leaders to school. The Catholic charismatic renewal is hardly being accountable to its own membership and to the Church when it takes no thought about obtaining proper certification for its educators, guides, counselors, and directors, in accord with the practice of other religious societies and as this kind of training becomes possible.

Official Status

General and special spiritual direction practiced in prayer groups and communities are charisms and ministries, but they are not offices in the Church. The Catholic charismatic renewal is not an ecclesiastical organization, a Church institution. It originates in the action of the Spirit and relates to the institution of the Church, but it is not part of the institution.[23] Thus it has its own loosely structured hierarchy of leadership, selected through various kinds of leaders' discernment. It might be considered a domestic Church, an *ecclesiola* or living unit of the *Ecclesia,* but as of now it has not been structured into the Church. Canonically, it has the status of "a good work"; practically, it enjoys a healthy relationship with ecclesiastical authority.

The ministries of direction within the renewal are thus private matters. Spiritual direction within the Church has never been tied into ordination; lay persons exercise spiritual direction and allied functions as well as do ordained ministers. In the past such ministry was frequently connected with the office of superior, and it was always considered as being necessarily charismatic, that is, it had to be under the influence of charisms in order to be valid ministry in the Church.[24] From Paul's time onward the Church oversaw the exercise of these functions (1Cor 14,37; 1Cor 1,10). The Church is the final arbiter of the validity of the charism (*Lumen Gentium 12*). It must "protect the genuine charisms against pseudo-charisms and unhealthy phenomena, and maintain the community in the good order which the charisms themselves are meant to serve (1Cor 14,33)."[25]

Prayer groups and communities do well to work in close contact with the hierarchy in order to maintain and foster their informal identification with the Church. They do this by relating to the bishop of the place, either personally or through his liaison or the local pastors. These nonofficial tie-ins are prudent safeguards against divisiveness, fragmentation, and unhealthy separation from the total Body of Christ.

Obedience and Submission

Both those who give and those who receive direction are subject to the higher authority of the Church. Their relation to the Church is properly one of obedience to the proper authority. The relationship of spiritual direction, therefore, is one that should remain within appropriate limits.

Within the renewal itself, do those in submission to designated heads owe a similar obedience to these leaders? Must the members obey the coordinators of the community? Do members of a prayer group owe obedience to the group itself or to its recognized leaders? What is the proper relationship between shepherd and sheep in the Catholic charismatic renewal?

I submit that obedience in the proper sense does not enter this picture. Submission and docility are the qualities called forth from those who voluntarily choose to belong to a prayer group or a covenant community. This means that members willingly submit to the group and its organizational structures, and that they are docile, that is, teachable. But per se they undertake no obligation of obedience to the group or to its leadership.

Leaders of such groups do not belong to the chain of command in the Church which is the vertical line of authority that gives jurisdiction or dominative power. Leaders in the renewal and spiritual directors in general are receivers of God's word and grace, fellow searchers with their people for God's will. They stand in the center among their brothers and sisters and relate on the horizontal level to one another. Their leadership takes on a jurisdictional or dominative character by being inserted into the official structure of the Church, as happens in religious or secular institutes.

Religious subjects practice a similar horizontal submission. For them, though, it is obedience, since they are inserted into Church structure. This obedience is said to be dialogic, and the dialogue continues between superior and subject as long as the matter warrants. Subjects have their say, indeed they have the second to the last word, but the superior has the last word. Any legitimate (juridic) superior, such as a father in the family or a teacher in the classroom, enjoys the same kind of right and duty. In the renewal the leaders and spiritual directors have the last word only in the sense that they can terminate the relationship in the presence of intractable or otherwise unreasonable opposition.

The "authority" of a spiritual director in both the general

SPIRITUAL DIRECTION

and special functions does not exceed that of a freely recognized competency. The director-directee relationship is not egalitarian. Neither is it master-disciple in an authoritarian sense, nor father-son in a juridic sense, nor superior-subject in a canonical sense. It is an informal, freely negotiated authority that is sui generis. This fact seems to have been questioned by one side in the recent shepherding-discipleship-submission controversy.[26] Spiritual directors, as well as guidance persons, pastoral leaders, and individual counselors, work in tacit submission to the authority of the teaching, ruling, and sanctifying power of the Church, an authority which is not likely to assert itself except in a crisis situation.

The authority given to leaders in the charismatic renewal is not jurisdiction in the Church, but authority in its etymological sense of "enabling to grow." This power to serve is really given to the leaders by the members. It includes both the external ordering of the group and the personal lives of individuals to the extent that these areas are committed to the pastoral care and/or spiritual direction of the leadership. Such authority is as strong as the agreement, and binds in conscience according to the intentions of both parties to the contract.

Leaders should not exceed their competence or invade privacy. It would be well for all concerned to recognize the distinct areas or forums of the exercise of leadership in order to safeguard the rights of secrecy and confidentiality. The external forum has to do with the general or public good, the administration of the prayer group or community. The internal forum is the realm of conscience. Information that comes out of personal counseling sessions, private guidance, or spiritual direction in the strict sense belongs to the internal forum and is an entrusted secret. In between these two areas is the paternal forum. Here the leader is acting as a father, not as a judge; his concern is the private interest of the individual, not the good order of the group. As a leader he receives privileged information that belongs to the private life of the individual, for example, his health or family situation. What he learns here is confidential and cannot be divulged or used for public decisions in the external forum in any way that would compromise the person.

The renewal tends to blur these three forums. An example is the preference for reducing both general and special spiritual direction to one overall, single relationship, that of the head or spiritual elder. Speaking of introducing the concept of headship and submission into religious life, Fr. George Kosicki writes:

> In the past we had separated the roles of superior, confessor, and spiritual director so that the superior was not to involve himself in the spiritual life of the individual and the spiritual director or confessor was not to involve himself in the daily life of the individual. We need to recover the role of a 'spiritual elder' who would take responsibility for the whole welfare of the person. Each person needs such a 'head' to reflect his needs, to challenge him, to confront him with his agreements, to foster his total growth.[27]

This is a return to an earlier historical pattern of the relationship between the public and private sectors of a person's life.

This history is usually written in terms of the practice of manifestation of conscience.[28] From the beginning, manifestation of conscience to a spiritual father was strongly urged, and choosing an appropriate confidant with great care was wisely emphasized. Isaias the Abbot, who was active around the year 488, forbade self-revelation to an ignorant or imprudent person—this implies that Isaias had no magic concept of obedience or discernment.[29] Benedict legislated the practice of manifestation of conscience into his Rule (chapters seven and forty-six); the abbot was the "spiritual father." St. Ignatius Loyola capped a long tradition when he made obligatory manifestation a key exercise, having in view both personal direction and the public administration of the Society of Jesus.

His original group of nine rules to govern the Society contained this prescription:

> They [the members of the Society] are to see in their Superiors the Image of God himself, assured that obedience is a guide which cannot be misled. They are to reveal all their thoughts as well as actions to those appointed over them, knowing that we must ever mistrust our own judgment.[30]

Safeguards were taken by the Society and there was an awareness of possible abuses of the practice. The practice persisted, however, and spread to many religious institutes until the mid-nineteenth century, when the Church frowned upon the mandatory manifestation of conscience and directed religious institutes to delete the prescription from their constitutions. In 1890, the Church totally abrogated the practice for lay communities.[31] The Code of Canon Law extended the abrogation to clerical institutions as well. In today's religious groups the superior and the spiritual director are usually distinct persons, even though the Code allows and even encourages the free manifestation of conscience to the religious superior. The renewal must be careful not to demand manifestation of conscience. But in promoting such manifestation, as it seems to do in "full submission headship" or in looking to elders for overall concern over one's life, the charismatic renewal should at least be aware of the history of this practice.

Communal Discernment

One feature that is truly a new form of spiritual direction in the renewal is the process of communal discernment at prayer meetings.[32] The whole group discerns the truth of a given proposed action, not by a process of majority vote, but by the group experience. The community is lifted up in praise, worship, and love of God. The pervading sense of presence and peace plus a deep solidarity in Jesus Christ is the backdrop on which the community senses the consonance or dissonance of a particular action: whether, for example, a speaker, a prophecy, or an announced decision is really "in the Lord." This is charismatic communal discernment.

This kind of discernment presupposes a mature group that has achieved a sense of community through sharing and praying as a body. The gifts are then operative and the discernment takes place not by the one gift of discernment of spirits, but by a convergence of many gifts, as William Spohn explains:

> In a charismatic prayer meeting, teachings, exhortations, prophecies and practical suggestions are advanced to seek the discernment which lies in the Body of Christ. No single individual possesses all the gifts of the Spirit, or has an infallible private index for his every inspiration. As in the Ignatian formula, the leading of one person should be expected to converge with the leadings of the Spirit expressed through others. One would be reluctant to accept one course of action, no matter how strongly proposed or received by the individual, if it failed to achieve congruence with the other gifts in the community.[33]

Spohn rightly argues that this is no mere discernment in accord with the rules of the "First Week" of the *Spiritual Exercises,* wherein general teaching is elaborated and applied to specific cases. Ignatian indifference is demanded here, and the election is made on the principles of the "Second Week." The dynamic of achieving group indifference is basically the same as that of the private disposition, namely the action of the Spirit of God. The group dynamic, however, is more dependent on the manifestation of complementary gifts.

George Montague corroborates this observation by describing a self-contained experience of special spiritual direction in the Corinthian Church:

It is of great importance to note that in the Corinthian community, where a strong central authority had not yet been established (other than Paul's at a distance), the gifts provided complementary controls of one another; tongues solicited interpretation. Interpretation rendered tongues intelligible, prophecy brought a fresh meaning of the word, discernment checked the authenticity of prophecy and so on. To what else can be ascribed the miraculous survival of the headless enthusiastic community than to the complementary interaction of the gifts of the Spirit.[34]

Is this group discernment a method which supplants individual, one-to-one spiritual direction? Is the method self-sufficent? The answer to both these questions, in my opinion, is no.

All discernment, whether individual or group, needs to be constantly open both to further discernment from the outside and to being checked from time to time. Occasionally, at least, it is wise for a person's spiritual director (who may be an elder or a head in the community) to check out his practice of spiritual direction with his own mentor or even with an outside expert, or through study of the professional literature. Such corroboration is elementary wisdom and occurs in all the professions. Leaders do well, therefore, to compare notes at regional conferences and study weeks, or by consultation with other sources (including noncharismatic ones) to insure the truth and prudence of their groups' discernment.

Individual direction is still indicated for those who practice group discernment, and this for two reasons. First, groups that are able to rise to the level of the God-experience and that are involved in group discernment are spiritually mature. Such groups do exist, but realistically they are hard to find. Most groups leave some margin of possible error in this kind of group discernment because of their own immaturities.

Secondly, group discernment would seem to apply to group

decisions and not to the concrete singulars for each individual. Individuals within the group still have their own spirits to objectify and judge their personal call and response in the context of the community judgment. The correct discernment of the group leaves room for each person's further election. Only individual discernment will uncover the special, personal aspects, and for this to happen, individual spiritual direction is necessary. A case in point would be someone who enthusiastically embarks on an otherwise good community program, but is carried away by immoderate zeal and lack of sufficient knowledge of himself and his project to such an extent that he may be harming the community program and other personal obligations. "Zeal without knowledge corrupts," and individual knowledge comes through individual discernment.

Charismatic Spiritual Directors

Need the individual personal director of charismatic persons be charismatic himself? Obviously, there is an advantage if the director is part of the renewal. But as long as he has experience and knowledge to understand the working of God in the charismatic renewal, he is qualified as a spiritual director. There are some advantages if he is a "loving critic" of the renewal because he thereby offers a sobering influence and perhaps greater objectivity. It is important that spiritual directors in the renewal have more than just the charismatic experience to recommend them. They best serve the renewal by being aware of the whole tradition of the Church and not just the slice of Christian history which began at the turn of the century in Kansas or in 1967 at Duquesne.

The validity of this observation may be illustrated by comparing the traditional attitude and the attitude of the renewal with regard to charismatic gifts. The renewal thrives on the gifts; it welcomes them, seeks them out, loves to express them. This is because the charisms are visible manifestations of the Spirit of God for the building up of the Body of Christ.

They are social and ministerial in nature.[35]

The mystical tradition of the Church, on the other hand, seems to take a different view of the charisms. Here the viewpoint is personal union with God, and the charisms as such are peripheral to that union. They do disclose the action of the Spirit, but they are not the Spirit himself. Hence, they are not to be compared to faith, hope, and charity which are the proximate means of union with God. In case of danger to the purity of these theological virtues and within the context of personal sanctification, the charisms are pushed into the background. What they bear, according to John of the Cross, is already accomplished by the time they are consciously recognized.[36] They are a hazard in the unpurified person because he tends to latch on to them over and against the deeper reality of union with God. He is in danger of putting the gifts ahead of the Giver, preferring the visible manifestation of the Spirit to the Spirit himself.

At first sight there is a contradiction in these two approaches. But, as the Malines Document rightly observes, "One does not apply the norms of mystical theology in the same way to mystical experience as to charismatic experience."[37] Mystical experience is interior and personal; charismatic experience is social and ministerial. St. Paul lays down pastoral guidelines for the assembly exercising the charismatic or ministerial gifts; John of the Cross is concerned about the inexorable demands of the personal ascent of Mount Carmel. They are speaking in different contexts. When they move to the same perspective, however, they agree. Paul's message in 1Cor 13 is a caveat for the exercise of the charismatic gifts; this message is the central theme of the teaching of John of the Cross. Both saints are pastoral and pragmatic, but they are addressing different situations. A knowledge of both teachings will temper the attitudes of the charismatic leader and the spiritual director in their respective roles.

Conclusion

Spiritual direction, both general and special, is basically the same in and outside the Catholic charismatic renewal. More spiritual direction is taking place (and by different agencies) in the renewal than in ordinary Catholic life, but the principles which elucidate it are the same for all. The experience of the direct action of the Spirit does not replace direction; rather, direction becomes more necessary, both in terms of a basic Christian indoctrination and human maturation, and in the actual work of discernment. The charismatic renewal is one spirituality in the Church at the present moment, often opting pragmatically for a particular approach to various issues in the Christian life. This is an acceptable course of action for any voluntary group. It must, however, endeavor to make the best choices. A knowledge of history may well moderate some judgments, and leaders at least should be as aware as possible of other viable options for living out the full Christian life. The Spirit has always used human instruments in his work, and the better equipped the spiritual teachers, counselors, leaders, and directors can be in experience, knowledge, and prudence, the more the renewal will flourish.

NOTES

1. The concept of spiritual direction is basically the same both in Eastern and Western Christian tradition. The delineation of the role, however, varies considerably from age to age and between Western and Eastern authors. Thomas Merton, in his *Spiritual Direction and Meditation* (Collegeville: 1960), and "The Spiritual Father in the Desert Tradition" in *The R.M. Bucke Memorial Society Newsletter-Review,* Vol. 3 (Spring, 1968), pp. 7-21, as well as Jean LaPlace, S.J., *The Direction of Conscience* (New York: 1967) expose the same tradition as Kallistos Ware, "The Spiritual Father in Orthodox Christianity," *Cross Currents,* Vol. 24(Summer/Fall, 1974), pp. 296-313. But their points of emphasis, their language and literary style, the "Western" effort to "rationalize," that is, render a reasonable account of the faith process and integrate it with contemporary anthropology and psychology, as compared with K. Ware's style of heightening the mystery and the transcendent quality of spiritual direction, lead to different "models" and even understandings of the same reality. Our bias in this article is the "Western" exposition of writers like Merton and LaPlace.
2. Ep. 87, 7 in *P.L.* 182, 215, cited by P. Pourrat, "Direction spirituelle," in the encyclopedia *Catholicisme* 4, pt. 1, p. 866.
3. In *Acte et documenta congressus generalis de statibus perfectionis, Rome, 1950,* (Rome: 1952) 2, 713, 714.
4. "The Need for Direction," *The Way,* Vol. 2 (July, 1962), pp. 163-165. Walsh's views stirred up a storm of disagreement among readers of *America* magazine, in the issues of 107 (12 October, 1962), pp. 877-879; 107(20 October, 1962), pp. 931-932; 107(10 November, 1962), pp. 1016-1018; and 108 (January, 1963), pp. 58-59.
5. T. Schaefer, O.F.M. Cap., *De Religiosis* (Rome: 1947), n. 684, cited by John C. Ford, S.J., "Religious Superiors, Subjects and Psychiatrists," *Proceedings of the Catholic Theological Society of America,* Vol. 17(1962), p. 96.
6. Herbert F. Smith, S.J., "The Nature and Value of a Directed Retreat," in *Review for Religious,* Vol. 32(1973), pp. 493-494.

7. Graham Pulkingham, "To Know and Be Known," in *Pastoral Renewal,* Vol. 1(August, 1976), pp. 9-12.
8. John Welch, O. Carm., "Formation as Orchestration," in *Review for Religious,* Vol. 34(1975), p. 925.
9. See Bert Ghezzi, *Build With the Lord* (Ann Arbor: Word of Life, 1976), p. 47.
10. David L. Fleming, S.J., "Models of Spiritual Direction," *Review for Religious,* Vol. 34(1975), pp. 352-353.
11. Hans Urs von Balthasar, "Immediate Relationship with God," *Concilium,* Vol. 29(New York: 1967), p. 51.
12. *The Spiritual Exercises of St. Ignatius,* n. 18.
13. Jacques Leclercq, "The Priest Today," *Review for Religious,* Vol. 22(1963), pp. 157-171.
14. E.E. Larkin, O. Carm., "Spiritual Direction Today," *American Ecclesiastical Review* (September, 1969), pp. 204-210, especially pp. 206-209.
15. Henri J.M. Nouwen, *The Genesee Diary* (Garden City: 1976), pp. xii-xiii. Other recent authors intimate a preference for a less directive attitude on the part of the director. Sandra M. Schneiders, I.H.M., for example, will sustain the title "direction" only if it refers to the thrust or orientation of a life, the final cause of the relationship and not an activity of either party. "The Contemporary Ministry of Spiritual Direction," *Chicago Studies,* Vol. 15(1976), p. 123.
16. Friedrich Wulf, "Spiritual Direction," *Sacramentum Mundi,* Vol. 6, p. 165. The word "specifically" is my own addition.
17. K. Truhlar, S.J., *Problemata theologica de vita spirituali* (Rome: 1960), pp. 108ff.
18. See *The Book of Her Life,* tr. K. Kavanaugh, O.C.D., and Otilio Rodriguez, O.C.D. (Washington, D.C.: 1976), c. 13, nn. 16-20, pp. 94-96.
19. J.D.Futrell, S.J., "Communal Discernment," *Studies in the Spirituality of the Jesuits,* Vol. 4 (November, 1972), n. 5; L. Orsy, S.J., "Towards a Theological Evaluation of Communal Discernment," *Studies in the Spirituality of the Jesuits,* Vol. 5 (October, 1973), n. 5.
20. Fleming, *op. cit.,* pp. 355-356. For example, "Direction . . . is seen in its ordinariness of one man helping another to clarify and objectify God's will in his life" (p. 356).

21. R. Kiefer, book reviews of J. Fichter, Cardinal Suenens, K. McDonnell, and others, *Commonweal,* (March 26, 1976), p. 214: "The movement thrives on association among charismatics . . . Immense energy is devoted to instruction and counseling."
22. One priest-psychiatrist arguing from an awareness of the harm that can be done due to an ignorance of psychology has recently suggested that "spiritual counselors should be required to undergo examination and have their knowledge and competence certified, the way pastoral counselors, teachers, psychologists, and psychiatrists are." James J. Gill, S.J., "Psychiatry, Psychology and Spirituality Today," *Chicago Studies,* Vol. 15 (1976), p. 37.
23. A paradigm of a healthy relationship between the charismatic movement and the larger Church is the fourth century "ascetic movement," in which there was recognition of "unordained elders" by both sides and the full integration of the ascetic movement into the whole Church by the ordination of one elder. See Stephen B. Clark, *Unordained Elders and Renewal Communities* (New York: Paulist Press, 1976).
24. K. Rahner, S.J., "Charism," *Encyclopedia of Theology, the Concise Sacramentum Mundi* (New York: 1975), p. 184.
25. O. Semmelroth, "Ecclesiastical Office: II, Office and Charism," *Sacramentum Mundi,* Vol. 3, p. 172.
26. Erling Jorstad, "Agenda for Charismatic Renewal," *The Ecumenist,* Vol. 14(January-February, 1976), pp. 29-30; Edward E. Plowman, "The Deepening Rift in the Charismatic Movement," *Christianity Today* (October 10, 1975), pp. 52-54. A group of thirty-eight charismatic leaders representing the broad spectrum of the movement in the United States met at Oklahoma City, March 8-12, 1976, and ratified the "Ann Arbor Statement" (December 16-17, 1975), which affirmed a basic unity as well as recognized differences. The differences, it was stated, were "well within the bounds of 'allowable variety' in the body of Christ."
27. "Renewed Religious Communities: the Dynamics of Rediscovery," *Review for Religious,* Vol. 35(1976), pp. 22-23.
28. Dacian Dee, O.F.M. Cap., *The Manifestation of Conscience,* CUA Canon Law Studies, n. 410, (Washington, D.C.: 1960), pp. 1-30; Dacian Dee, O.F.M. Cap., "Manifestation of Consci-

ence," *New Catholic Encyclopedia,* Vol. 9, pp. 160-161; Francis N. Korth, S.J., *The Evolution of 'Manifestation of Conscience' in Religious Rules III-XVI Centuries* (Rome: 1949).
29. Dee, *op. cit.,* p. 11.
30. *Ibid,* p. 24.
31. Decree "Quemadmodum," issued in 1890 and cited in full in Dee, *op. cit.,* pp. 91-93. Canon 530 of the Code of Canon Law contains the present legislation.
32. For an excellent description and evaluation of this process, see William C. Spohn, "Charismatic Communal Discernment and Ignatian Communities," *The Way Supplement,* n. 20 (Autumn, 1973), pp. 38-54.
33. *Ibid,* p. 45.
34. George Montague, S.M., *The Spirit and His Gifts* (New York: 1974), p. 38.
35. *Theological and Pastoral Orientations on the Catholic Charismatic Renewal* (Malines: 1974), pp. 4,12, and passim.
36. *Ascent of Mount Carmel,* pp. 2, 17, 7-9, *The Collected Works of St. John of the Cross,* trans. Kieran Kavanaugh, O.C.D., and Otilio Rodriguez, O.C.D. (Washington, D.C.: 1973), pp. 158-159.
37. Malines document, p. 24. See also Peter Hocken, "Pentecostals on Paper," *Clergy Review,* (November, 1974), p. 767.

A RESPONSE TO ERNEST LARKIN'S PAPER
Robert L. Faricy, S.J.

We need, and the Church in general and charismatic renewal in particular need, the clear thinking on spiritual direction that Fr. Larkin's paper expresses. He makes some necessary distinctions, and he stresses the continuity between the Church's tradition of spiritual direction and spiritual direction in the charismatic renewal today. With the idea of complementing what Fr. Larkin has done, I would like to speak more in terms of concrete personal experience where distinctions sometimes get blurred; and I would like to stress the discontinuity between spiritual direction as I have found it in the charismatic renewal and outside of the renewal. My method will not be that of systematic spiritual theology, but rather that of describing briefly my own experience—what I have learned—in giving spiritual direction before I began to participate in charismatic renewal, and after.

My experience has been not so much in general spiritual direction, which would include pastoral counseling, individual guidance, and spiritual government, as it has been in the area of spiritual direction properly so-called—the kind that centers on the God-dimension, that has as its focus a person's relationship with the Lord, and the direction in which the Lord is leading. I have found that this spiritual direction takes place as much in informal situations as it does in more specific situations; I often find myself in a helping relationship centered on a person's relationship with the Lord simply in ordinary conversation.

When I first began to give spiritual direction, the first thing I learned was to listen, and to listen carefully. By careful listening I mean listening with care, in a caring way, with interest and with love. It is not only a question of knowing the facts by listening to what is said, but also of hearing what lies behind what is said, of hearing how the person feels about the facts. Learning to listen takes some time and discipline, but besides being absolutely necessary for both informal and more formal spiritual direction, it leads one to take people more seriously. And this leads to much, especially regarding those persons whom almost no one takes seriously and few really listen to, children for example.

In spiritual direction, listening to what another person says goes together with listening to the Lord, with a prayerful openness to God at the time on the part of the director. This is because the real spiritual director is always the Lord himself. And it is only to the extent that he is present in the relationship between the two people who are talking that anything profitable can take place. The term "spiritual direction" is of course a misnomer. A spiritual director's job is not so much to direct as to help another person find out what the Lord wants, what direction the Lord is giving and wants to give to the person.

Listening, obviously, is not enough; dialogue must take place, especially so that the person who in some way is looking for direction can be helped to be honest with himself or herself and with God. It is so easy to make compromises and then to dishonestly justify those compromises in the name of freedom or growth or overwork or the new theology or whatever. Dialogue can bring the dishonest justifications or compromises to light, sometimes in their very beginnings.

This should be enough to indicate how I gave spiritual direction before entering the charismatic renewal. I still do the same things now, but, in general, things seem to move much faster. I also do a number of things that I did not do before, or that I did not do to the same degree. In particular, I pray with people more than I used to. For example, I will pray aloud with someone for some specific need. It might be that the need is for greater stability and fidelity in one's personal prayer, or for greater love and openness toward those in one's family or community, or for an increase in the charism of consecrated celibacy, or for peace, or simply for a greater surrender to the Lord in some part or in the totality of one's life. I pray in faith, trusting in the Lord's promise that if two or three are gathered together in his name they can ask for whatever they need and he will answer their prayer. I might pray for interior healing: for healing of the heart in some particular area, for the healing of one or more hurtful memories, for a removal of bitterness or resentment or sadness. On a few occasions I have prayed for deliverance. I sometimes pray with a person so that the person might be free from some specific bondage. Often, especially before praying for inner healing, I help the one with whom I'm praying to forgive others, to renounce any sins or sinful tendencies or situations, to be sorry for them, and to ask the Lord's forgiveness. Since being baptized in the Spirit, I depend more on the Lord for knowing what to say and do, and for knowing what to pray for.

Spiritual direction is, always, not just one person seeking help from another, but—in a deeper and truer sense—two people going together to the Lord on behalf of one of them in order to seek the Lord's will, his strength, his guidance, and his gifts. In the case of spiritual direction within the context of the charismatic renewal, I find that this going-together-to-the-Lord becomes radically more real, more actual, and more efficacious. There is less dialogue between the other person and me, usually just what seems necessary, and more dialogue between us and the Lord. This, and the greater evidence of the power of the Lord's love, accounts for most of the difference between spiritual direction as I have experienced it outside of and within the charismatic renewal.

In fact, I am more certain than ever that what is basic to spiritual direction is love: responding in a union of love with another to the Lord's love for us both, and letting the Lord's love flow into the spiritual direction relationship and operate there. Love is "the most excellent way" (ICor 12,31) in spiritual direction as in other matters. It is well to know what to pray for and how to pray for it, to be able to listen, to have some knowledge and experience of the spiritual life. But the main thing that I have learned is the overarching importance of letting the healing and saving power of Jesus' love move through me to the other person.

A RESPONSE TO ERNEST LARKIN'S PAPER
Judith C. Tydings

In my response to Fr. Larkin's paper within the time-limit prescribed, I would like to take up four basic points: 1) superiors and spiritual direction; 2) obedience, *de facto* and *de iure;* 3) the place of baptism in the Spirit; 4) community and commitment.

Superiors and Spiritual Direction

Fr. Larkin states:

> Superior and spiritual director were united in the one office during the middle years of the Church, and there was then no distinction in practice between the internal and external forum. The two areas were separated by the Irish monks in the seventh century when they connected spiritual direction with confession.

The underlying assumption throughout Fr. Larkin's presentation appears to be that the increasing separation betwen the exercise of authority and the giving of spiritual direction represents continuous progress, that the Church has gone from good to better to best. The truth might be exactly the reverse—we may have gone from best to worst! And I would suggest that this separation may have been a direct consequence of the loss of a sense of Christian community.[1]

St. Vincent de Paul did not regard this separation as ideal. In a conference he gave in January, 1658, St. Vincent talked to his Daughters of Charity on the subject of who they should approach to discuss their temptations. He said that it would ruin their Company if they were at liberty to confide in whomsoever they pleased.² He tells the Daughters to turn to their superior:

> Why do you think you are recommended to turn to your Superiors? It is because just as the head conveys spirit and life to all the members of the body, so Companies should receive from God, through their Superiors, all the graces of which they stand in need. If your arm was injured and another person's arm was taken and lent to you, would it receive the necessary influence whereby it would act like all the other members? No, because it is the head which gives spirit and life to the members that are united to it. So resolve then to be very exact about this rule. If you do otherwise, it is to be feared that you have been badly advised. You will turn to someone who knows nothing about your spirit. He may say to you: 'O sister, since this is so, it is quite impossible to live with people of such discordant characters. If your trouble arises from this, O sister, leave the Community.' And there you have the poor girl in danger of losing her vocation.³

In speaking of early monastic practice Fr. Larkin rightly remarks that the spiritual father and superior was "a transmitter of life." Fr. Sullivan said much the same thing about the Apostles and St. Paul in his paper on Tradition. Paul told people to imitate him and they did so. Spiritual fathers were imitated. The Apostles, St. Paul, spiritual fathers, and all our saints have been transmitters of life. In the Eastern Church, spiritual fatherhood was exercised by the elders or "old men," who were known by the Russians as a "starets" and by the Greeks as a *Geron*.⁴

The Christian communities emerging from the charismatic

renewal are providing spiritual fathers. Those who have founded Christian communities and those who hold positions of responsibility in such communities are transmitters of life. And all, to my knowledge, unite headship and direction.

In my experience, the separation between authority and direction hinders growth in the Spirit. I would say that there are very few dynamic spiritual directors in the Church today. In the charismatic renewal, particularly in communities (and Fr. Larkin's paper unfortunately doesn't really advert to the differences between spiritual direction in prayer groups and such direction within covenant communities), I see people being healed, loved, cared for, and supported. I see people being directed, guided, and formed. I see lives being changed. I don't see this happening as consistently, as well, or as fast, anywhere other than in the communities arising out of the charismatic renewal. Theologians might well ask why the spiritual direction being exercised in the renewal, particularly in communities, is so much more effective than the other forms of direction being given in today's Church.[5]

Obedience, *de facto* and *de iure*

Fr. Larkin argues that "obedience in the proper sense does not enter this picture," that is, enter into any relationship between leaders and "led" in the renewal. But later he says, "Religious subjects practice a similar horizontal submission. For them, though, it is obedience . . ." He seems to be saying that no covenant community could require obedience of its members until it were formally recognized by the Church in some way, for example, by designation as a secular institute.

This is to deny *de facto* obedience until there is *de iure* obedience. But an examination of the history of religious orders and institutes in the Church would show that obedience, just as poverty and chastity, was there from the beginning of a foundation. The Jesuits were practicing obedience well before the Society received its formal approval from the Pope.

The Place of Baptism in the Spirit

This is the most important point I want to make. Fr. Larkin's paper does not once mention "baptism in the Spirit." But baptism in the Spirit is so foundational to the charismatic renewal, and thereby to any spiritual direction in the renewal, that its omission from this paper is not only surprising—it puts into question the adequacy of Fr. Larkin's main contentions.

This should serve as a real caution with regard to the danger of becoming so caught up with formation and growth that we forget how to initiate people into the Christian life. We can lose baptism in the Spirit if we are not careful—and we could wind up all over again being God's grandsons instead of his sons.

An understanding of baptism in the Spirit and a knowledge of a person's spiritual state at the time of his or her baptism in the Spirit is necessary to the effective direction of those touched by the Holy Spirit in the charismatic renewal. Steve Clark has written something highly significant in this regard.[6] To my knowledge only one theologian (Fr. Piet Schoonenberg) studying this topic has commented on this and taken up Steve Clark's point:

> The Stephen Clark aforesaid points to the classic distinction between the way of purification, of illumination and of union. The usual notion, but not the only one, is that these ways follow the one upon the other . . . There can however be a different way; in fact it happens differently in the pentecostal experience. 'The difference between what is happening now in the charismatic renewal and what happened in some traditional forms of spirituality is that in the charismatic renewal, people are being baptized in the Spirit at the beginning of their spiritual growth.'[7]

We can learn much from spiritual theologians such as Garrigou-Lagrange, Tanquerey, and de Guibert. However, we have to know how to place baptism in the Spirit within their framework. I believe baptism in the Spirit to be a unitive experience that can happen at any stage in the spiritual life, or even before a spiritual life begins. I have developed these points in my book, *Gathering a People*.[8]

Community and Commitment

I have already remarked that Fr. Larkin's paper does not sufficiently distinguish what is happening in charismatic communities from what is happening in charismatic prayer groups. I believe that baptism in the Spirit is meant to be an initiation into community life, and that the gifts of the Spirit are meant to be exercised in a communal context. And so I would believe (and I know from my own experience) that effective spiritual direction in the renewal as well as in the Church takes place in committed relationships within Christian community.[9] If this has always been true, it is even more so today.

Pastoral leaders in the renewal can only benefit from good theology. But good theology assisting God's work in the renewal can only be produced by those who have an accurate knowledge of what is at the heart of the charismatic renewal, and this by being in touch with what God is really saying and doing. As I believe that the formation of Christian community is central to the charismatic renewal, it is important for the theology of those involved in the renewal that theologians have an understanding of the communities arising there. I would therefore strongly recommend that theologians spend some time participating in the life of such communities.

NOTES

1. The separation betwen superiors and spiritual directors no doubt acted as a safeguard against authoritarian abuses once community and sharing in spiritual leadership had broken down.
2. Some might think that St. Vincent's desire to prevent his Daughters from associating with nuns, convents, and monasteries was aimed at ensuring that his women wouldn't get enclosed in the same way that St. Francis de Sales' Visitation sisters had been. I think that a good case can be made for the view that he didn't want his Daughters confused or tempted by contact with lax religious life.
3. *The Conferences of St. Vincent de Paul to the Sisters of Charity,* trans. Rev. Joseph Leonard, C.M., Vol. IV, pp. 78-79.
4. "The importance of obedience to a *Geron* is underlined from the first emergence of monasticism in the Christian East. St. Antony of Egypt said: 'So far as possible, for every step that a monk takes, for every drop of water that he drinks in his cell, he should entrust the decision to the Old Men . . .'" Kallistos Ware, "The Spiritual Father in Orthodox Christianity," *Cross Currents,* Summer-Fall 1974.
5. I can speak with the greatest confidence and a knowledge of the forms of spiritual direction given in my own community, Mother of God in Potomac, Maryland.
6. Steve Clark, *Baptized in the Spirit* (Pecos: Dove Publications, 1969), pp. 87-96.
7. P. Schoonenberg, "Baptism with the Holy Spirit," *Concilium,* November/December 1974, p. 30.
8. Published by Logos International, 1977. Cf. especially Appendix I.
9. In order to be effectively directed, it is recommended (though not considered essential) to live in a household, as other forms of commitment are possible there. For those not part of a household, the Mother of God community provides other ways to have a committed relationship to the community.

THE ROLE OF TRADITION
Francis A. Sullivan, S.J.

Tradition

In the early 1960's three important steps were taken toward a common understanding among Catholics and Protestants of the role of Tradition in the preservation and interpretation of the gospel. The first was the publication of Yves Congar's two-volume, historical and theological study entitled *La Tradition et les traditions*. The second was the Report of the Fourth World Conference on Faith and Order (held at Montreal in 1963) concerning "Scripture, Tradition and Traditions." The third was the promulgation in 1965 of the Second Vatican Council's *Dogmatic Constitution on Divine Revelation*, with its treatment of Tradition in the crucial second chapter, "The Transmission of Divine Revelation."

While it would be overoptimistic to claim that by these three steps a perfect accord on the question of Tradition had been reached, still it is undeniable that they show a remarkable convergence in their approach to the basic question, "What do we mean when we talk about Tradition?" To begin with, they agree on what we do *not* mean by Tradition. They agree that the New Testament revelation cannot be conceived as part of a body of truths or propositions of faith, some of which were written down (in the New Testament) and others of which were not written down, but transmitted only by word of mouth until they eventually surfaced in Christian documents of later centuries. The New Testament revelation is instead, they agree, the total reality of Christ, the total experience of his disciples, all that they had heard, had seen with their eyes, had looked upon and touched with their hands, concerning the word of life (1Jn 1,1-3). Jesus Christ himself is the Word that God has revealed to men; he himself is the good news; his life, death, and resurrection, his glorification and lordship, his sending of his Spirit—all this is the gospel. The "full gospel" is not just words that could be spoken and written down; it is the full reality of Christ and his Spirit, of Easter and Pentecost.

And if the New Testament revelation is this total reality of Christ, as our three sources agree, they also agree that Christian Tradition is nothing less than this "full gospel," the Christ-event as experienced by the disciples, and as shared by them and thus handed on in and through the apostolic community. As the Faith and Order Statement of Montreal puts it, "Tradition is the Gospel itself, transmitted from generation to generation in and by the Church: Christ Himself present in the life of the Church."[1] The same statement goes on to specify how this transmission takes place:

> Tradition taken in this sense (as the Gospel transmitted in and by the Church) is actualized in the preaching of the Word, in the administration of the sacraments and worship, in Christian teaching and theology, and in mission and witness to Christ by the lives of the members of the Church.[2]

In a similar vein, the Second Vatican Council declares:

> Now what was handed on by the Apostles includes everything which contributes to the holiness of life and the increase in faith of the People of God: and so the Church, in her teaching, life and worship, perpetuates and hands on to all generations all that she herself is, all that she believes.[3]

There is agreement, therefore, that Tradition is not just a part of Christian revelation, consisting of some truths which did not happen to get written down in the New Testament. It is clear that Tradition is the full gospel, precisely as this was shared and handed on by the disciples to the Christian community, and as it has been transmitted from generation to generation in and by the Church. It is the whole gospel, and it has been proclaimed, believed, lived, professed, celebrated, and put into practice in the life and worship of the Christian Church. And it is in all of these ways that each generation of Christians has handed on the gospel to the next generation.

There is significant agreement also that this transmission of the gospel in and by the Church takes place "through the power of the Holy Spirit."[4] Or, as Yves Congar puts it, the Holy Spirit is the "subject" of Tradition, the one ultimately responsible for the purity and integrity of the gospel as handed on in the Church.[5]

Scripture and Tradition

In the light of the foregoing concept of Tradition we can now see that the New Testament is the privileged, divinely inspired written witness to first-century Christian tradition. It preserves for us, as only written documents can, a priceless and unchanging record of the recollections of the first disciples about Jesus, his words and actions, and of the faith that their testimony engendered in the Christian communities. Indeed, critical study of the New Testament makes it ever clearer to what extent these writings reflect the living, developing tradition of the gospel in the early Church; one can distinguish among different interpretations of the basic gospel message as it was being understood, lived, and handed down in different Christian communities.

One thing is clear: The New Testament is the written form of the same Tradition that was being expressed and transmitted in many other ways than by writing it down. The content of the one and of the other is the gospel itself, the reality of Christ and the redemption he has wrought. At this point it might be possible to ask, Once the New Testament had been written and the canon of its books had been settled, would the Tradition have any further function or use?

An answer that Catholics have sometimes given to this question is that Tradition has preserved for us some truths of the Christian faith which had been taught and handed on orally from the Apostles, but not included in the New Testament writings. It is now generally agreed that there are simply no truths of our faith that would fall into such a category.

On the other hand, what the Apostles did hand on, and what by its very nature could not be reduced to writing, was a whole way of living the Christian life. In the words of Paul to the Philippians, "What you have learned and received and heard and seen in me, do; and the God of peace will be with you" (Phil 4,9).

So the abiding function of Tradition consists in this: that as the New Testament is the written form of the gospel, so it is the same gospel as lived, understood, and handed down in the Christian community which offers the most reliable criterion for the interpretation of the written record, and its application to the ever-new problems that succeeding generations will have to face. As the New Testament is the "book of the Church," so it is that it is in the Church and under the guidance of the Holy Spirit promised to the Church that the New Testament witness to Christian tradition can best be understood.

Even on purely natural grounds one would expect that the written documents on which the life of a community is based would be best interpreted by the community that lives according to those writings, in the light of its own traditional way of understanding and practicing them. If this is true of *any* community, how much more is it true in the case of the Church, where we have the promise of Christ to send his Holy Spirit, the Spirit of truth, to abide with his Church and lead it into all truth.

There is broad agreement among Christians of many different confessions—though not of all—that this promised assistance of the Holy Spirit was effective in a particular way in those decisive interpretations of the gospel which were made in the light of Tradition by the great ecumenical Councils of the first millenium. For such Christians (including, of course, ourselves) such interpretations of the gospel not only were made in the light of Tradition (i.e. in the light of the Church's understanding and practice of its faith), but for succeeding generations have become elements of the Tradition by which scripture itself is to be understood. All Christians who accept the dogmas and creeds of the early Councils as binding for their faith do actually interpret scripture in the light of this Tradition, even though they may claim to accept the Bible as the sole rule of faith.

What distinguishes the Catholic understanding of Tradition from that of many other Christians is our belief that through their contemplation of the gospel and the intimate understanding of spiritual things which they gain through experience of them,[6] the faithful can be led by the Holy Spirit to a kind of intuition of aspects of the gospel which can be found neither explicitly in scripture, nor in the ancient sources of tradition, nor can they be rigorously deduced from these sources.

The Tradition and Traditions

The Montreal Faith and Order Report observes that the term "traditions" is currently used in two senses: to indicate particular expressions and manifestations of the one Tradition in diverse historical forms, and to indicate the various confessional or denominational traditions peculiar to the various Christian communions.

Congar also distinguishes between Tradition and traditions, but on somewhat different grounds; he is particularly concerned with determining what the Council of Trent meant by the "unwritten traditions." His conclusion is that the Tridentine Fathers had in mind various elements of Catholic belief and practice which, even though not explicitly mentioned in scripture, were of such venerable antiquity that they were taken to be of Apostolic origin. For the most part, the examples given in the writings of the period have to do with practice rather than belief, although some of them have important implications for the faith. An illustration of this would be the practice of baptizing infants. As proof that such an intuition is truly though only obscurely and implicitly contained in the gospel, Catholics require and accept as sufficient that 1) it is consonant with everything else in the gospel, and 2) that the whole Church has come to a firm and abiding belief that such a truth is really part of the gospel. The most obvious examples of such intuitions are our Catholic beliefs concerning such privileges of the Virgin Mary as her Immaculate Conception and Assumption into heaven.

The attitude of most Protestants is that these doctrines are peculiarly Catholic "traditions" which do not belong to Christian Tradition, taking this term to mean the gospel as transmitted in and by the Church. This leads us to consider the distinction that has to be made between Tradition and traditions.

Leaving aside the historical question of the interpretation of the Council of Trent (on which I am in agreement with the analysis given by Congar), I would like to consider a very crucial question raised by the Montreal Faith and Order Report. The question is this: By what criteria can we judge whether a particular tradition (some element of belief or practice that is traditional in a Christian Church) is really part of Tradition, that is, of the gospel itself, or at least is a legitimate expression of some aspect of the gospel? The Montreal Report asks, "Do all traditions which claim to be Christian contain the Tradition? How can we distinguish between traditions embodying the true Tradition and merely human tradition?"[7]

Cardinal Meyer raised substantially the same question in one of his interventions at the Second Vatican Council the following year. He observed that not everything that is traditional in the Church is necessarily a legitimate tradition; there can be a distorting as well as an authentic tradition. As examples of inauthentic traditions he mentioned a kind of piety that is contrary to the spirit of the liturgy, and a casuistic moralism. Consequently, he called for a recognition of the need to consider traditions critically and proposed scripture as a criterion for this indispensable criticism of traditions.[8]

J. Ratzinger, in his commentary on the *Dogmatic Constitution on Divine Revelation,* remarks that it is to be regretted that the suggestion of the American Cardinal was not taken up by the Council; in fact, he says that Vatican II more or less ignored the whole question of the criticism of tradition, thus missing an important opportunity for ecumenical dialogue.[9] The question of whether traditional beliefs and practices in the Church are subject to criticism and judgment by the criterion of scripture is a question that goes to the very heart of the Protestant Reformation. On the other hand, I think it can be said that while it did not express this in theory, Vatican II actually did put into practice such criticism and judgment with respect to certain traditions in the Catholic Church, and this in large measure on the basis of scripture.

As I see it, the difference that remains between a Catholic and a Protestant attitude on this question is this: Whereas a Protestant would tend to require some positive and explicit textual support from scripture to justify the acceptance of a tradition as belonging to "The Tradition," a Catholic would be satisfied by knowing that a tradition is thoroughly consonant and harmonious with the biblical sources, even though not explicitly mentioned in them. In other words, a Catholic would judge a particular tradition to be unscriptural only if it is out of harmony with scripture, and a Protestant would judge a tradition unscriptural merely because he finds no mention of it in scripture.

THEOLOGICAL REFLECTIONS
Denominational Traditions

The term "traditions" is used not only of particular Christian beliefs or practices, but also of those whole sets or complexes of traditional ways of understanding and practicing the faith which are distinctive to each of the Christian denominations. Thus one speaks of the Lutheran tradition, the Roman Catholic tradition, and the Anglican tradition. The Second Vatican Council uses the term in this way especially when speaking of the differences between the "Oriental" (the Eastern Orthodox) and the "Western" (the Roman Catholic) traditions. Thus, for instance, the Council says:

> In the investigation of revealed truth, East and West have used different methods and approaches in understanding and proclaiming divine things. It is hardly surprising then, if sometimes one tradition has come nearer than the other to an apt appreciation of certain aspects of a revealed mystery, or has expressed them in a clearer manner.[10]

Of course, the Council did not go so far as to say that perhaps in some instances the Lutheran or the Reformed traditions have come nearer than the Roman Catholic to an apt appreciation of certain aspects of a revealed mystery, or has expressed them in a clearer manner. But I do not know on what grounds one could rule out such a possiblity. In fact, it seems to me that the acceptance of such a possibility would be a basic presupposition for fruitful ecumenical dialogue.

In any case, what seems particularly significant for our present purpose is the observation made in the Montreal Faith and Order Report that all Christians, whether they are aware of it or not, tend to read and interpret scripture in the light of their own denominational traditions. The authors of the Report see important ecumenical progress in the fact that "we are more aware of our living in various confessional traditions e.g. of that stated paradoxically in the saying: 'It has been the tradition of my Church not to attribute any weight to tradition.' " The Report goes on to say:

> Loyalty to our confessional understanding of Holy Scripture produces both convergence and divergence in the interpretation of Scripture . . . How can we overcome the situation in which we all read Scripture in the light of our own traditions?[11]

I would like to offer some reflection on this question. First of all, I agree with the Report that it is an important step forward in ecumenical dialogue for Christians of all denominations—especially, perhaps, of those denominations that claim to recognize scripture alone as their authority in matters of faith—to become aware of the extent to which their interpretation of scripture is determined by their particular tradition. Awareness of this fact is not enough, however; awareness must lead to a greater effort to understand one's own tradition, and this, of course, involves the need to know what it has in common with other Christian traditions, and in what ways it is distinctive. Obviously, not everyone can be expected to acquire such knowledge, but it should at least be part of the education of those who are being prepared for ministry in the respective Churches.

But again, even such knowledge of one's own and other Christian traditions is insufficient. It must be joined to a critical judgment that is open to what is sound in traditions that differ from one's own, and is receptive to criticisms of one's own tradition, being able to weigh such criticism on the basis of objective criteria. But even granted the presence of such an open attitude of mind (which does not allow mere confessional loyalty to prejudge the issue), the problem still remains: What are the objective criteria on which such a critical examination of Christian traditions can be based?

I am sure that all Christians will agree that scripture is such a criterion. But after this has been agreed upon, there still remains the question of whether scripture is the *only* criterion on which a critical examination of Christian traditions can be based. Many Protestants would no doubt take this position. For Catholics, however, there remains the possiblity of weighing a particular tradition against the broader, more universal Christian Tradition.

An example of this might be the question of baptizing infants, where Catholics would criticize the Baptist tradition not only on the basis of scripture, but also, and even more importantly, on the basis of the antiquity and universality in both Eastern and Western Christendom (apart from the Baptists) of the tradition of baptizing the young children of Christian parents. In other words, for a Catholic it is possible to achieve certitude that a particular tradition is really part of the Tradition on other grounds than its explicit mention in scripture. In this stand our Orthodox brethren would surely be in agreement with us.

What is the basis of our certitude in such a case? It is our faith in the indefectibility of the Church, which would have grievously failed if through most of its history it had deprived most of its members of valid baptism by baptizing them in their infancy. And our faith in the indefectibility of the Church, in turn, is based on the promise of Christ to abide with his Church to the end of time and to send it the Holy Spirit, the Spirit of truth, to lead it into all truth. Here we arrive at what is perhaps the most fundamental difference between a Catholic (including here the Orthodox) and a Protestant mentality, namely, the difference regarding their understanding of the relationship between the Holy Spirit and the Church.

To return to the question raised by the Montreal Faith and Order Report—"How can we overcome the situation in which we all read Scripture in the light of our traditions?"—I would answer that we should by all means read scripture in the light of our tradition, but under the following conditions:

1) that we make the needed effort to understand our traditions, both our own and those of other Christian communions,

2) that we are respectful of traditions, both our own and those of others, and give them proper weight in our interpretation of scripture, and

3) that we are also critical of traditions, being ready to examine and judge both our own and those of others, to determine as best we can whether they really belong to the great Christian Tradition, and to reform our traditions if need be.

The Role of Tradition in the Interpretation of the Pentecostal Experience

The early Pentecostals were biblical Christians who recognized scripture as the sole rule and authority in matters of faith. Instinctively, it was to the Bible that they looked for an interpretation of the religious experiences of Charles Parham and his students in 1901, and of the experiences of many hundreds of people during the Los Angeles revival of 1906. They undoubtedly thought it was from the Bible alone that they drew their interpretation of this experience as being the fulfillment for each Christian of the promise of Jesus that his disciples would be "baptized in the Holy Spirit" (Acts 1,5).

However, it is not difficult to show to what extent the early Pentecostals interpreted their experience in the light of their respective religious traditions. I say *respective traditions* because while practically all early Pentecostals came from an Evangelical Protestant background, they were more or less equally divided between people from the Holiness tradition, and Evangelicals such as Baptists and others who did not accept the Holiness teaching about a "second blessing" which brought about "entire sanctification." In the Pentecostal interpretation of their new experience, one can see the influence, first of their common Evangelical tradition, and secondly of their respective traditions, whether Holiness or not Holiness in tendency.

The basic tenet of Evangelical Protestantism concerns the necessity of a personal experience of conversion to Christ in order to gain salvation. The early Pentecostals all had such an experience, and they all believed themselves saved. Their new religious experience, manifested by tongues and other signs, was therefore something that happened subsequent to conversion—in fact, years afterward for many of them. It was inevitable, therefore, that they interpreted this as a "second blessing," distinct from and subsequent to conversion, and that they looked in the New Testament to find such a pattern of religious experience. Indeed, they thought they found it there, not only in the case of the Samaritans converted and baptized by Philip (who still had to wait for the coming of the Holy Spirit), but as the normal experience of all New Testament Christians. Thus the Pentecostals thought they were drawing from scripture alone their distinctive doctrine according to which a Christian, already converted to Christ and baptized, must wait and pray until he receives his "baptism in the Holy Spirit," his personal Pentecost.

One can easily see that the Pentecostals' stress on the importance of personal religious experience, and their interpretation of "baptism in the Holy Spirit" as an experience, necessarily distinct from and subsequent to conversion, owes much to their common Evangelical tradition.

But many of the early Pentecostals also came out of the Holiness tradition which had already taught them to look for a "second blessing" subsequent to conversion which would accomplish their "entire sanctification." Such people, who believed that they had already had their second blessing and who now recognized their pentecostal experience as something new and distinct, naturally concluded that the complete Christian life must include all three experiences, with the "baptism in the Spirit" as the third and crowning blessing to be sought. This is the teaching of the Pentecostal-Holiness Churches, whereas Pentecostals not of the Holiness tradition look on sanctification either as a work of God in the soul "completed" at conversion, or as a gradual growth in holiness throughout Christian life.

I think it is clear that the interpretation given by the early Pentecostals to their religious experience owes much to their respective traditions, notwithstanding their own profession to accept the Bible as the sole authority in matters of faith. Indeed, it was inevitable that this should have been the case, since it is equally inevitable that every Christian with a denominational background will tend to interpret scripture itself in the light of his denominational tradition, whether he is aware of the extent to which he is doing so or not.

One practical conclusion that follows from this is that there is a real and important distinction to be made between the "pentecostal experience" as such, and the typical Evangelical Protestant interpretation which the early Pentecostals gave to it, and which has become the accepted teaching of the Pentecostal Churches. There is no reason why Christians of other and richer traditions, who come into this kind of religious experience, should rest content with the early Pentecostals' interpretation of it.

On the contrary, there is every reason why they should seek to interpret it in the light of their own traditions, as well as in the light of the best scriptural exegesis—in which, again, one must agree that the early Pentecostals are not the best guides to follow. The fact that the pentecostal experience can be fruitfully interpreted in the light of other Christian traditions—a fact which I believe is becoming more and more clear— suggests that it is a basically *Christian* experience, and not something distinctively Evangelical Protestant.

At the same time, in the process of interpreting the pentecostal experience in the light of our own traditions, we also have to avoid the danger of so "domesticating" it as to recognize in it only what we ourselves have had all along, with the danger of eliminating what is most vital in this movement and what could be its most important contribution to the renewal of ourselves and our Church.

There is now a Pentecostal tradition in Christianity by which our own tradition can be enriched; but we have to discern where the wealth of the Pentecostal tradition really lies. Surely it is not in its theology or exegesis; rather, its richness is to be found in its openness to the powerful working of the Spirit through the whole community, its participative and creative worship, its extraordinary effectiveness in communicating the good news of Jesus Christ. It is in these areas that the Pentecostals are leading the way, and that we of the more venerable and "respectable" Christian traditions must have the humility to learn and to follow.

NOTES

1. *Report of the Fourth World Conference on Faith and Order, Montreal, 1963*, ed. P.C. Rodger and L. Vischer (New York and London: 1964), p. 50.
2. *Ibid.,* p. 52.
3. *Dogmatic Constitution on Divine Revelation (Dei Verbum)*, n. 8, in *The Documents of Vatican II,* ed. Walter M. Abbot, S.J. (New York: The America Press, 1966), p. 116.
4. *Montreal Report,* p. 52.
5. Yves Congar, "Essai théologique," *La Tradition et les traditions,* Vol. II (Paris: Fayard, 1963), pp. 101-108.
6. *Dei Verbum,* n. 8, Abbot, p. 116.
7. *Montreal Report,* p. 52.
8. Quoted from the official Latin text of the Second Vatican Council, Vol. III, Part III, p. 150-151.
9. *Commentary on the Documents of Vatican II,* ed. H. Vorgrimler, Vol. III (New York and London: 1963), p. 185.
10. *Decree on Ecumenism (Unitatis Redintegratio),* n. 17, Abbott, p. 360.
11. *Montreal Report,* p. 53-54.

A RESPONSE TO FRANCIS SULLIVAN'S PAPER

Richard M. Liddy

Francis Sullivan's paper was an excellent presentation of the meaning and meanings of tradition. Two points caught my attention, one more subjective, the other more objective.

First of all, from the viewpoint of theological method (and in connection with Francis Martin's remarks on hermeneutics), I would call attention to Fr. Sullivan's quote from the Second Vatican Council's *Dogmatic Constitution on Divine Revelation* which speaks of the faithful appropriating tradition through a certain intuition or spiritual sense, "through the intimate understanding of spiritual things they experience" (Ch. 2,8).

All of us here, I believe, know what this means. It refers to the inner personal experience of the Holy Spirit by which we "sense" or "feel" the guidance of the Holy Spirit in our lives. It is this experience by which we are guided in choosing one direction in preference to another, one community life-style instead of another. It is according to this dimension of our experience that we see the presence of Jesus in our lives.

Now my observation is this: It would be a major breakthrough in clear communication if we could find a common theological language to relate this dimension of our experience to the various other levels of our experience and consciousness. Such a language can be a bridge between Christian and Spirit-filled experience and the many varied contemporary experiences and sciences of the human family. Without such a language-awareness, Christians run the risk of talking to themselves. With such a "transcultural" language the Holy Spirit can use Christian speakers and writers as channels to the many cultures and experiences of our day. Such a language would be an interiorly and personally appropriated anthropology that would function in conjunction with Christian spiritual experience as a basic hermeneutical principle for interpreting Christian experience and Christian meaning for persons of our day. "The Spirit as experienced" is the basic principle of hermeneutics, but that experience must be expressed in the words of a particular culture and in such a way, not just to challenge that culture, but also to build bridges to it. I might mention that Bernard Lonergan's work on the levels of human and spiritual consciousness in his *Method in Theology* has tremendous ecumenical implications in creating just such a language.

My second observation concerns more the objective notion of tradition which Fr. Sullivan sees in the living Christian community as the basic public and objective principle in interpreting scripture. The life of the living Body of Christ is the basic principle for understanding the meaning of scripture.

For a Catholic Christian such a living community involves various elements, not all of which he necessarily appreciates at once, some of which he must learn from others to appreciate, some of which as inauthentic "traditions" he is called upon to drop, but much of which corresponds to the "full gospel" he wishes to espouse and proclaim. This is Tradition with a capital "T." Living Christian faith in the Lord Jesus brings with it an appreciation of historically established beliefs and doctrines, communal sacramental or bodily piety, the centrality of the Eucharist, exigent moral demands, reverence for Mary and the saints of particular cultures, an order and structure of authority and direction, a reverence for intellect within the wider life of community (including today the Church's formal acceptance in Vatican II of the historical and human sciences in the critique of inauthentic traditions), etc. Integral to Catholic interpretation of Tradition is the belief that elements explicitly developing later in history can be authentic criteria for interpreting earlier elements (cf. Cardinal Newman on the development of doctrine).

Consequently, as we speak of the living Tradition of the Church as the principle for interpreting scripture, and though one local Church might emphasize one element over another, still it is one living Body with a dynamic harmony or proportion between all the elements. The symbol of the Body of Christ is important here, for as the human body lives under one principle while moving and developing its various parts, so the Body of Christ under the guidance of the Holy Spirit moves, acts, and develops often in one area at a time, but in no way cut off from union with the one life of the one Christian Tradition, Catholic in the best sense of the term. As St. Irenaeus put it, "Where the Church is, there is the Spirit of God; and where the Spirit of God is, there is the Church and every grace." My plea in this regard would be, as we emphasize one dimension of the Body of Christ in history (e.g. our particular vibrant community life), to be constantly aware of other dimensions, theological and pastoral, that contribute to this one Body in history.

THE RELATIONSHIP BETWEEN CHARISMATIC AUTHORITY AND CHURCH OFFICE

John C. Haughey, S.J.

I think it would be fruitful for us to "cross-rough" (a bridge word that seems apropos) the relationship between the power that comes from charism and the power that comes from office in the Church. I believe it would be fruitful not only because it is an interesting theological subject, which it is, but because a greater vitality for both the Church and the charismatic movement can come from an understanding of these two power realities in the Church. When their interaction is poorly understood, the result is abrasion. Later in the paper, I would like to talk about the authority of powerlessness, for it seems to me that the sinfulness in all of us comes out much more clearly when power is present—as it most certainly is in several different senses, in the charismatic renewal.

I will not dwell on the subject of office very long. I mean by it what you and almost everybody else have commonly understood it to mean when applied to the Church. It stems from or is traced in some way to the Apostles and is connected with the sacrament of Orders. Concretely, we are talking about the papacy, episcopacy, and priesthood, and all the analogous positions and responsibilities that are related to them. We are talking about the power to act officially in the name of the Church, whether that action refers to teaching, administrating, governing, "binding and loosing," or similar functions. There are many theological questions attached to each of these statements, but we will take the meaning of office in its common and traditionally accepted sense.

Charism, on the other hand, is more difficult to locate. It belongs, as Karl Rahner would say, to the most incalculable part of the life of the Church.[1] For that reason it has been aptly defined by no one. It can be viewed in the widest possible sense and, therefore, include office; or in the narrowest sense and connote only marginal and extraordinary phenomena. The apostle Paul from whom all analyses of charism stem, certainly does not give us the last word on it; he is not as interested in defining the charismata as he is in creating the criterion for their legitimacy. This criterion is, do they serve to build up the Church?

My own intention here is simply to give a behavioral description of charism. The charismata are those powers manifest in individual Christians which are not traceable to the fact of office or the conferral of any powers of jurisdiction on these individuals by the Church. Those who are endowed with such powers manifest them by the ability they have through their gifts to positively influence the religious, social, and moral behavior of others. They trace their ability to influence others not to themselves, but to God. Those who are led by the Spirit of God become respositories of some of the powers by which God would have his people strengthened. Those powers can be slight or mighty. In either case the "led"—those who are led by the Spirit of God—become in some way leaders. A charismatic person, in brief, is in this sense capable of being a leader, i.e. influential in affecting others' behavior.

The Relationship Between Office and Charism

Protestant ecclesiology tends to play office off against charism, the idea being that the Spirit operates in the latter but not in the former. However, the usual Roman Catholic understanding of the relationship between office and charism is that the one is intrinsically related to the other. These two sources of power, operating in and through individuals in the Church, are both from the Spirit. Like Paul, the Catholic understanding of Church sees it as "built upon the foundation of the apostles and the prophets" (Eph 2,20). Extend, so to speak, apostles and one comes to office; extend prophets and one comes to charismata. The Church is shaped by both these forms of authority and power.

The theological presumption is that since there is only one Lord and one Spirit, where there is division and conflict between God's several instruments it is not the Lord and his Spirit who are operating. Nonetheless, it is not true that all tension is unworthy of Christians. If there is no tension between these two kinds of power there is no growth. Tension is both a sign of growth and the immediate cause for the evolution of the structures of power in the Church. A pilgrim people has to have pilgrim structures.

Formal authority and charismatic authority need one another as a check and balance. Office without the pressure of charism against it becomes rigid. Charism without the stability of office becomes anarchy. The history of Christianity has been pockmarked with conflict rather than constructive tension whenever there has been an attempt to deny the validity of the dialectic from one or the other of these two forms of authority.

The two are not wholly dissociable. Some who hold authority by reason of their office influence the behavior of others only by reason of their office; others are influential due to the gifts evident in their persons over and above their office. Pope John XXIII is an evident example of the latter, but by no means the only one. One could list hundreds of bishops the world over whose power to influence their people is much more charismatic than it is due to the office they occupy. By the same token, one could inquire whether the sine qua non of the recognition of their charismatic gifts isn't their office, etc.

The formal authority of the Church would be wrongly

viewed if it were seen as the enemy of the charisms, even though there has been no small amount of obtuse handling of them by Church authority in the past. But it must be clearly stated again that the conviction that office is outside the Spirit whereas charism is in and of the Spirit is not Roman Catholic doctrine. At any given time, either or both can be "outside the Spirit." But as Rahner says, "Ultimately speaking the gifts of the Spirit can only be regulated by a gift of the Spirit."[2] By this latter "gift" Rahner is referring to the Spirit's functioning in office. In brief, office needs charism and charism, office. Charismatic authority unrelated to formal, ecclesial authority can become off-kilter just as surely as formal authority that is not aerated regularly by charismatic authority gets rigid and renders the Body of Christ listless and apathetic.

In fact, it could be argued that the best measure of the correct exercise of office is whether the charismata flow from the faithful to whom those in office minister. But when the faithful have been so gifted they stand in no less need of formal authority than before. Who of us in the renewal hasn't learned that charisms are often putative rather than actual, imitated rather than received? Self-appointed ministers of God's word can create enormous confusion when they speak from a universe of unsuspected or unadmitted ignorance. Prophecies, like the inspiration of scripture itself, are knee-deep in subjective elements that at any one moment can be in the ascendancy. What community can we point to in the charismatic movement that has not been afflicted for a brief or a long period of time with self-appointed teachers rampaging through it, propelled by their own needs, prattling formalae that they've memorized or heard or read, rather than things that they have been taught in and by the Spirit of God? Charismatics might be prone to see formal authority in the Church in a negative rather than a positive light, but if profound misapprehension about God's will and God's word were to overtake some portion of the renewal, howsoever unlikely that might be, its distortions could wreak havoc on untold numbers of the

CHARISMATIC AUTHORITY

faithful. The need for this other gift of the Spirit would be seen then in a new light as providing a counterbalance if exceptional circumstances were to develop.

When the charismata develop properly they seek or come from a communal base. This, in turn, has to formalize its own internal authority. In other words, charismata in any abundance grow toward formal authority in several ways. They cannot long endure in harmony or power unless they submit to or create their own formal authority. Steve Clark has treated one aspect of this theme well in his *Unordained Elders and Renewal Communities* (New York: Paulist Press, 1976), where he shows how the authority created internally by Christian communities was again and again accepted by the Church and fitted into the formal structures and offices of the Church.

In order to be a group, any group has to undergo an internal process whereby it deputes its own leaders and formalizes its leaders' authority. We do not exhaust the realities of power, authority, and leadership by dividing them into formal or juridical and charismatic. There is a third kind: leadership or authority that becomes formal inside a group, but is not related to formal authority outside itself. The stability of an emerging group, in other words, is not built solely on charismata, since in the natural process of social development as an organized entity it creates its own structures and appoints its own heads, the charisms notwithstanding.

These two different kinds of spiritual empowerments in the Church make it more likely that each will operate in a way that makes the Lord more transparent. It seems that they operate almost dialectically, keeping each other in line, so to speak. Left to itself, either charism or office can easily be turned into something that exists for itself, something that calls attention to itself or overestimates its own importance or becomes a source of privilege or status. Power has always been a dangerous commodity in the human order; it so easily begins for the sake of others and ends for the sake of the one exercising it.

Bernard Lonergan has an interesting essay on the subject of authority in which he traces the legitimacy of its exercise to the quality of authenticity.[3] Authenticity he sees as precarious and cumulative. The dialectic is between the authority that resides inalienably in the community, and the authorities who have been entrusted with certain powers by the community. Authenticity or inauthenticity can be found in any one of three different carriers: the community, the authorities, individuals in the community subject to the authorities.

Given this frame of reference, several remarks by Karl Rahner become interesting. He suggests that the future of the teaching office of the Church will be in the direction of a more radical witness to the substance of the truths of the faith already known, rather than in explicating more of these truths.[4] He suggests, furthermore, that what the teaching authority of the Church now teaches must "speak" to those hearing it and be seen for its own intrinsic truth, rather than accepted simply because authority says this or that is so.[5] One could conclude that the Church must teach more charismatically, i.e. the teachers and the content of what they teach must be persuasive on the basis of its internal attractiveness, transparency, and authenticity.

The U.S. Catholic Charismatic Renewal

At this point I would like to be more specific by making a number of empirical observations in order to spell out how I see these two sources of power operating presently between the formal officeholding authorities in the Roman Catholic Church and Catholic charismatics and their communities in the United States.

First of all, the charismatic movement has been making it

quite clear in practice that religious leadership and Church office are not one and the same thing. So often those in office show no great capacity for leadership, and frequently those who display clear religious leadership, many of whom are in the charismatic movement, do not hold office in the Church. If one concurs with what has been said above about charismatic leadership being the capacity to positively influence the religious behavior of others, then one would have to concede that charisms must in some sense contain their own power or be self-authorizing up to a point, at least. Furthermore, the authority of a charismatic person is vested in him or her by those whom they influence. It is equally true to say, of course, that the authority of charismatic leaders originates not so much from the people who perceive their special gifts, but from the gifts themselves and the Spirit who is their author.

Parenthetically it may be noted that what is true of individual charismatics is also true of charismatic communities. Whole communities come into being and begin to show a communal charism, and hence irradiate a certain authority. Since these display a capacity to influence the behavior of countless individuals and communities, they fit our descriptive definition of charism. Like the religious orders in the past, which through their charismatic founders began to diffuse their own unique charisms in the overall Body of Christ, these communities can operate as leaders in the same way as individual persons who are leaders. By extension, we should also say that the whole neo-pentecostal movement itself—insofar as it is a single discernible entity in and of itself—has manifested a capacity to influence the behavior of the rest of the Church. From this we see the propriety of its name, "charismatic movement."

A second observation: If the charismata are dispensed by the Spirit to build up the community of believers, and then given a movement which both preaches the divine intention to flood the Church with gifts (charismata) and proceeds to implement what it preaches, no wonder the formal authority of the Church is beginning in some places to feel itself being pressed, nudged, recontoured. Partly due to the charismatic movement, but even more so to other factors, those holding formal authority are being pushed to revalorize their authority. The revalorization to which they are being pushed is that of adding leadership to office, charism to juridical power, and the authority of gift to the fact of their office. These discomforting nudges from charismatic authority have been given to formal authorities throughout the history of the Church, but the modern situation seems to be more pointed and ubiquitous, possibly because there is such a wide disaffection in all structures of society with those who hold power by reason of office. Maybe the Spirit of God himself shares in the disaffection, since almost overnight the Spirit has created a whole infrastructure of "saints" who operate in a quasi-public way by reason of the capacity that so many of them manifest to influence others' behavior by what they are and what they do or say, in the area of healing, counseling, confronting, etc. The *anointeds* are having the effect that was once expected and allowed only from the *appointeds*. This has been happening during the last ten years in this country, at least, in a quiet way and without any great conflict. And that is as it should be, if both groups have power from the same Spirit.

A third observation: For charismatics, the function of formal authority in the Church becomes simultaneously more important and less important. It becomes more important because when Jesus gains in being Lord of the many aspects of the renewed Christian's life, then anything or anyone that enfleshes his will or presence becomes more and more estimable. But since the Roman Catholic understanding of "Church" has always seen the Apostles and their successors and those commissioned by the successors of the Apostles as standing in the place of Christ and expressing his will for his

Body, those in office become increasingly important. At the same time, formal authority becomes less important because determinations for action, mission, and ministry now come much more pointedly and frequently from inside the hearts and minds of the renewed Christians, as a result of their experience and attunement with the Spirit. (I am not talking about something wholly new, of course, but the depth and breadth of this is new.)

A renewed Church becomes more charismatic, and a charismatic Church perceives authority as co-extensive with the Body of Christ. When there are a number of Christians maturing to the point of ministerial efficacy, juridical authority has the happy responsibility (not a new one in kind, but in degree) of having to coordinate the charisms evident in the members of the Body of Christ—not to mention having to consolidate, harness, and correct them. How much more like the Body of Christ to have bishops, popes, and pastors in that position, rather than the one that they have known too often in the past of speaking to relatively inert flesh (at least publically inert, since it seemed obscene for the personal charisms of the faithful to have a public airing)! It seems only right that the responsibility of formal authority be in the area of exercising a unitive, directional, and confirming role, rather than an initiating or baptizing one.

That role is the easier one for formal authorities to accept. Less comfortable is the nudge that charismatics tend to impose on those in office which might be described as the primacy of the experiential. In effect, charismatics imply that the authority of those in office must be revalorized by the religious experience of the officeholder. When Jesus is experienced as Lord, he is experienced as disseminating power. Matthew's Jesus claims that all power in heaven and earth is now concentrated in his person (Mt 28, 18-20). If one pauses over that text, one sees that it suggests that Jesus' commissioning of his followers does not result in their possessing his authority, but rather their exercising his authority which never becomes theirs. He commissions a power to be used in his name which does not cease to be his power.

All authority which comes from Christ (it is perhaps careless to speak of it as being "in the Church") functions to generate two experiences in the faithful: the experience of sonship—knowing who one is with a self-understanding born of the Spirit—and of empowerment. But one or both of these cannot take hold of any percentage of Christians without that portion of the Body of Christ of which they are a part undergoing a recontouring at the level of power. Powers then permeate the Church. These two experiences are at the root of the purpose and credibility of authority, both for those exercising it and those on whom it is exercised. These experiences are shared by a growing number of the faithful, especially charismatics.

A fourth observation: Confusion results when charismatic authority fails to distinguish itself sufficiently from formal Church authority. Charismatic authority misinterprets its nature when it attempts to influence behavior by binding those under it to courses of action as if it were office or by taking upon itself a degree of permanence that is not assured by any charism.

In the sense in which we have spoken here, how long does a leader remain a leader? Many who show the gift of leadership and make themselves instrumental in renewing persons and communities in the Church can be tempted to use their gifts long after they have run out. Charismatic leadership is not automatically extended by God to an individual on a lifetime basis. The capacity to discern in one's self or in charismatic communities the temporary nature of leadership gifts can be very freeing for people and communities. In the absence of such discernment, and given the presence of dependency-prone people who are anxious to confer authority on those who either do not have it or do not have it for life, the situation of whole prayer groups and residential communities is exacerbated so that their harmonious functioning becomes problematic. Even without being aware of it, those with charismatic authority (no less than those with juridical authority) can begin to use their authority as if it were a possession and begin to deal with those they have influenced in the past as if they had some proprietary rights over their lives. If the Master was tempted, as he was, to use for their own sake the extraordinary gifts that he possessed, the disciple should expect to be tempted in the same way.

More study needs to be done on the question of charism. Two recent authors have seen charism more as an event than as a permanent power. According to Schweizer, it is an experience of God's *charis,* his gracious love, for the time and only for the time that the affected person experiences it.[6] Since it is not "mine," but always for the other, it cannot be made to function with the same degree of stability and permanence as office. I only want to report this here and not claim to know what this means in practice when, for example, members of a community feel called to make a permanent commitment to charismatic groups in which stability is a necessity.

Closely connected to this issue of the permanence and impermanence of charisms are two other points that I would like to make. With regard to the first, there seems to be talk in the renewal about the renewal being oriented to and for the Church, taking place in the Church, and eventually disappearing. But there seems to be little preparation for what this means in practice. When is the task of charismatic leadership that of preparing for its own disappearance? If the timing is not discerned accurately, the premature fadeaway of charismatic leadership can leave the marriage between Christ and that portion of his people affected by the renewal precarious. On the other hand, when the fadeaway is overdue, the community that should have been incorporated into the structural life of the Church remains ectopically positioned in the Body of

Christ, unable to vitalize the Body or be vitalized by it.

The second issue has to do with the permanent commitment made by individuals in covenant communities that are not yet formally related to the Church. It would seem that the permanent commitment of at least Roman Catholic Christians to covenant communities requires that these communities eventually be in some relationship to formal authority outside themselves. It does not seem possible that Catholic Christians could commit themselves to a community in the Body of Christ if that community, in turn, never determines or is unclear about its relation to that Body.

But this remark only opens up the issue and must be connected with the fact that the residential or covenant charismatic communities are of great importance for the ecumenical movement in this country. They have the advantage of and the responsibility for creating new wineskins for the new wine the Lord is lavishing on his people. They are for the same reason at a disadvantage and peculiarly vulnerable because these interfaith, covenant communities represent a new thing. They do not fit into the old wineskins—the canonical categories of yesteryear—and if forced to fit into them, will either not survive or will lose the promise they represent.

Bishops and charismatic leaders have to keep interweaving two disparate strands to make prudent judgments about these communities. One of these strands has to do with time, the other with the exceptional character of covenant communities. It takes time for Christians in these communities to sort out their respective calls; on the bases of these individual "sortings-out," communities come to understand to what extent they are being called into communal life and, in turn, are able to discuss what their mission is. There is a time lag between the moment of the individual's discernment of God's call to the community and the community's understanding of its relationship to the Church. This is not unusual and has happened in almost every instance in which a religious congregation came into existence in the history of the Church.

CHARISMATIC AUTHORITY

What is unusual at present is that Christians from different denominations and Churches are doing this discerning.

With regard to the second strand, it would be absurd to say that such groups are illegitimate because they have not come into existence in the past. In general, it seems to me that there has been a happy degree of openness and mutual respect between bishops and charismatic leaders thus far concerning the exceptional nature of covenant communities. I have no information, furthermore, that leads me to think that there is or will be conflict between the residential charismatic communities in this country, which have a large percentage of Catholics in their membership, and the bishops of the dioceses within which those communities are growing. This is as it should be, since these communities could have a very important role to play in the wider future ecumenical shape of the Church of Christ. That having been said, however, it is important for charismatic leaders to remember that Roman Catholics cannot bind themselves forever to a community in the Body of Christ that intends to leave forever indeterminate its own relationship to the visible, social, institutional reality in that Body which is the Roman Catholic Church.

A fifth observation: The relationship between charismatic authority and formal authority turns sour if the former begins to be the judge of the latter and presumes "to sit on the chair of Moses" and, at least in effect, assume some of the responsibilities of those in formal authority. More specifically, some charismatics seem to presume to know that certain congregations or parishes of the Church are not renewable or that certain religious orders are not renewable. There is no charismatic gift that allows one to judge whether a brother or sister, or a community or a parish or a congregation is not renewable. It is one thing to be led by the Spirit in a given direction, but quite another to judge as being unrenewable those to whom one is not led. Furthermore, it is unconscionable to dampen the ardor of someone who is attempting to discern the presence of a religious or priestly vocation by suggesting that these vocations "are not where it's at," since the Lord is instead "doing a mighty thing among us," thereby implying that "he's no longer doing it among 'them.'"

This observation leads us to a more generic remark. There will be no tension between formal Church authority and charismatic authority for those who have consciously or unconsciously subscribed to an anabaptist concept of Church, since the only authority in such a Church is charismatic. Charismatic authority takes on all the functions that the Catholic concept of Church considers proper to office.

Let me point out some discrepancies that gradually begin to develop when the ecclesiological intake of Catholics is at variance with their own Church's understanding of itself. These are not things that I have dreamed up, but things that you and I have heard from too many Catholic charismatics. There is no lack of faith nor is there ill will in judgments such as these, but they furnish us with evidence that a non-Catholic criteriology has begun to develop, albeit unreflectively, when such ideas as the following are propounded: "Conscious fellowship creates the Church"; "The ecclesiastical reality that antedated the charismatic movement was devoid of the charisms; it was not of the Spirit, and not yet the Church"; "Teaching that does not derive from personal experience cannot be authentic"; "The present congregations of the faithful contain only potential members of the authentic, Spirit-filled Church, rather than true members of the body of Christ."

Left without proper teaching, Catholic charismatics can unsuspectingly subscribe to an ecclesiology that is at odds with that of their Church. Such an ecclesiology is prevalent in some of the pentecostal literature that in so many other aspects speaks effectively to the experience of Roman Catholic charismatics. When the framework within which one's experience is interpreted is a revivalist, noninstitutional, privatistic ecclesiology such as pentecostal literature frequently develops, the danger is great that the experiential will run amok.

Essential to Catholic spiritual formation, it seems to me, is the Eucharist. The Eucharist teaches by symbol, among other things, the nature of the Church. A community that is Eucharist-centered is not likely to misconstrue its place in the Church; the community can be taught its place daily. This is perhaps the most awkward aspect of the life of these new charismatic covenant communities. They have inherited most strikingly the division of the Body of Christ and give great promise of reknitting it in places. Lacking the possibility of celebrating and receiving the Eucharist all together, they miss this symbolic source of unity. Therefore, the source of their banding together is much more Word-centered than Eucharist-centered. The fault for this is not theirs of course, and they need to be encouraged by formal authorities to plunge on in their attempts to live the unity that we Christians already have in Christ, even though the members of their communities do not all come from the same ecclesial tradition.

The Authority of Powerlessness

I would now like to say a few things about a subject that those who hold formal authority in the Church, as well as those who exercise their charisms in a way that influences others, can't hear enough about. The charismatic renewal has had a marvelous effect on the Church in this country because it has not only reminded us of, but manifested the degree of power that Jesus would have his followers proclaim and exercise. Powers that had up until the recent past been considered part of the mythological past of the Church are now seen as not quite so mythological after all, since they are exhibited in the lives of so many people in the renewal. But immediately we come to the paradox that runs all the way to the core of the gospel: the paradox of powerlessness. The Christian faith calls one to powers and powerlessness, self-emptying and being filled at the same time. This paradox is most difficult to perceive (as well as live by) in relationship to authority, both for those holding authority and those under authority in the Church.

As the charismatic renewal grows and deepens, the paradox becomes more difficult, rather than less difficult, to embrace. There is a greater respectability now in the general Christian population for the charismatic renewal, and hence there is a greater respectability attached to those who locally or nationally are seen to be members of or leaders in the renewal. Praise God for that, of course, except that the likelihood of a mixture of motives on the part of actual or aspiring leaders is greater in this new situation. It is also true that it is always difficult for any movement to pass from the first generation to the second generation of leadership. Handing on responsibility has been problematic in the human order ever since society came to be. To put the point more strongly: The charismatic renewal in its macro and micro-structures in this country has arrived at a power moment. What is crucial now is that it traverse this moment according to the gospel way of looking at power rather than in any worldly way.

What I would like to do in this section, therefore, is to analyze the experience of powerlessness both as lived by Jesus and taught by him. The servant cannot hope to be greater than the master, and if the master accepted, chose, adopted, or experienced the situation of powerlessness within which he would exercise his power, the servant must do the same to be faithful as well as credible. The forms of power that I have in mind which must be suffused with the lesson of powerlessness are all those whith which the Lord endows his people in the new creation: charismata, *exousia,* offices, and *dunameis.*[7] Each of these must be exercised in a radically different way than their counterparts were exercised in the old creation.

There were two distinct moments mentioned in the synoptic gospels when Jesus taught his followers the disparity between the way in which he measured importance and power and authority, and the way in which his contemporaries measured these things. When his followers wanted to know the measure of greatness in the kingdom that he was proclaiming, he called a child into their midst and indicated that "unless you turn and become like children, you will never enter the kingdom of heaven. Whoever humbles himself like this child, he is the greatest in the kingdom of heaven" (Mt 18,3-4). Stature or importance is to be measured in Jesus' kingdom not by position or power or visibility, etc., but by one's characterological resemblance to a child.

Jesus did not use a child as the image on which he wanted his followers to focus because he saw a child as innocent—Jews did not so look upon childhood. Rather, he used the image of child as dependent and powerless. This is what the child experiences and this is what Jesus made the ideal for his followers: chosen, accepted, adopted powerlessness. This was so contrary to the measure of importance that his own and any other culture used that it represented a clear mutation in religious, political, social, and cultural values. One thinks again of Isaiah's "My thoughts are not your thoughts and my ways are not your ways"—so different is the new creation to be from the old. Choose and accept the fact, Jesus is saying, that all of God's actions upon us are in function of fashioning us as children, his children. This is the image in the Divine Artist's mind according to which he works. Jesus is not talking about an ethical ideal, but is giving a picture of what faith-power fully responded to will do. "To all who received him . . . he gave power to become children . . ." (Jn 1,12). If we let God have his way, then each of us becomes more and more childlike.

The ideal of childlikeness acts as a magnet around which so many other evangelical ideals and counsels can be grouped. For example, the description of mission that Jesus envisions his followers to be undertaking suggests "take nothing for the journey." That is to say, externalize your interior state of childlike trust in God and entrustment of yourself into his hands by not having tangible things to reinforce you in your mission. The absence of externals on which to rely will be both an expression of your dependency on God, and a reminder of it. Thus to "sell what you have . . ." is an invitation to the same kind of childlike trust so that it is God alone on which one relies. Jesus, of course, invited his followers to become like him in all of these things rather than to conform to some ideal or norm abstracted from him. That is to say, he himself embodies the ideals he preaches. Jesus, when seen in all his childlikeness, reveals himself as totally dependent on the Father with whom he identifies. He does not see himself as a vine detached from the soil any more than he sees his followers as branches detachable from himself, the vine.

Jesus lived in the experiences of both power—being empowered—and powerlessness, leading to trust. What he continually attempts to convince his hearers is that—it works! Hence his concern to wean them from trusting themselves surrounded by things that in turn become the objects of their anxiety. He tells them: You are putting your trust in things that can't come through for you; put it in the only one who can, my Father.

This ideal to which God calls the Christian also constitutes the agenda for authority in the Church. Childlike dependence on the Father and on the one whom he has sent is the aspiration that every exercise of authority in the Church must reinforce. Since the description of the kind of personhood the Spirit is empowering is "childlikeness," so all authorities in the Church must exercise their offices and gifts to the same end and purpose.

What characterizes a child is, among other things, single-mindedness—not in the sense of a virtue, but in the sense of awareness of oneself as lost outside of the range of one's parents' protection. A leader, in turn, is childlike in his leadership when all of his power is exercised single-mindedly, that is to say, when he lives in an awareness of the fact that his whole being comes from God and is returning to God and is breathed into by God's own Spirit. All of his actions are an expression of that inspiration. Jesus' leadership was increasingly childlike as he grew in visibility in Palestinian society all the way to the point of the total entrustment of himself to his Father in the crucifixion.

There is still another description of what constitutes the greatest and most powerful person in the kingdom that Jesus proclaimed. "Whoever would be great among you must be your servant, and whoever would be first among you must be slave of all" (Mk 10,43-44). As with the previous image, this is not an ethical exhortation, but rather a description of the force called faith and where it takes one if one accedes to its power. The power of faith is given so that it might go out from oneself and bring the self-concerned self along with it. "Whoever would save his life will lose it; and whoever loses his life for my sake, he will save it" (Lk 9, 24). In Jesus' view the empowered person, the person empowered by God's own power, serves.

As always, we can see the lesson best in the case of Jesus' own life. Every exercise of power in his life was an act of service. The exercise of power par excellence was the laying down of his life freely. If one uses the capacity to influence the behavior of others as the measure of gift, power, and authority, then one would have to look to the crucifixion as the most powerful moment in all history because it is the most influential, because the most self-emptying. Jesus' freely chosen death is not an exceptional moment in his life, but rather the moment that expresses best the meaning of all previous acts in his life. What made Jesus' life exceptional was not only the powers he had (he received the power of the Spirit without reserve, as Jn 3,34 notes), but the way in which he used the powers that he had. Power went out from him, as the crucifixion itself shows; it went out from him to serve those for whom it was exercised. It was not power lost; it was power transmitted effecting transformation. The paradox between power and powerlessness in the new economy of salvation instituted by Christ will never be more simply exhibited than by the crucifixion scene. It says beyond the shadow of a doubt that powerlessness itself is power. It was Jesus' choice of powerlessness in obedience to his Father that made for the unparalleled explosion of spiritual power. The first effect of his freely-chosen powerlessness was an exaltation so high that Jesus arrived at a place no less exalted than the right hand of the Father, there to be Lord like the Father of all that ever was, is, or will be.

John's Gospel has plumbed the depths of the paradox even more than the synoptic accounts of the passion, death, and resurrection of Jesus have. John is anxious to show that Jesus' humiliation and descent into the depths is his glorification; his humiliation is his glorification, not just that which *led* to his glorification as the other evangelists have shown. That is to say, the act of losing one's life is the gaining of it, in this case, not only of eternal life, but of consubstantiality with the Father. This is a crucial lesson to learn because all of us have enough faith to know that God's power is made manifest in weakness or flows through the weakness of human flesh.

But what the crucifixion calls for is a further step: that we see that the reign of God is just as present in weakness and suffering and humiliation and death. God is reigning there, and his power is operating then no less than when a miracle is being performed. It is not that the cross leads to the resurrection and the glorification, but that resurrection power makes the cross glorious. The power of the resurrection breaks in from the future into the present suffering. Powerlessness itself is a sign of the presence of salvation, not the vestibule to it. Sometimes salvation's presence is manifested by signs of power, but more often by the sign of Jonah.

The gospel runs counter to all the attitudes that we naturally take concerning respectability, position, acknowledgement, importance, visibility, or their opposites. It flip-flops every one of these attitudes by insisting that all servants are the royalty and that all the biggies are of little importance. Small is beautiful, one might have the gospel say. This is the conversion to which every Christian is called in an ongoing way, but to which it is especially difficult for those to submit who have tasted respectability—including charismatics—not to mention visibility, acknowledgement, etc.

People in authority, whether charismatic or formal, who have not tasted the paradox of the gospel, are likely to succumb to the omnipresent human itch to run the lives of others in the name of service. The rhetoric of service has made serving respectable. But the rhetoric and the actual serving are obviously not one and the same reality. Service has become one of the more common forms, one of the more useful cosmetics, for attaining to and holding on to power for its own sake. Many who began as servants of the Lord in positions of authority end up creating conditions in which their own needs are operating quite as much as the needs of those whom they purport to serve.

One of the surer indications that this process is occurring is rigidity about how service will be undertaken, who will perform it, and what those who are served need (whether they know it or not). One of the best signs, in turn, that authority is being used for the benefit of those who are served rather than for the servants, or that power is going out from the servants to the served, is that the servants are flexible about the structures needed to serve. Since the needs of those who are served are diverse and evolving, the structures that exist to meet those needs must also be diverse and evolving. Furthermore, the served themselves will grow only insofar as they themselves are able to participate in the structures of service that all ecclesial authority must create. The Church has seen this lesson in increasing clarity, as the Second Vatican Council's collegiality insights attest.

I think the charismatic renewal in this country has been remarkable in the rapid evolution of structures that have been created to serve the thousands in whom the Spirit is experienced in a new way. What I'm suggesting here is that this evolution has been a good thing and shouldn't "plateau" now. The same prayerfulness that was the precondition for the first generation of structures is also needed for the second generation.

St. Paul has a few things to say about the subject of power and powerlessness which should serve to reinforce the preceding. Paul was an incredible repository of the powers with which God wished those cavorting around in the new creation to be endowed, and he exercised them unstintingly to serve the initial Christian communities that he was instrumental in setting up. At the same time, he refused to make use of these extraordinary powers in such a way that they would be made credible by their being packaged and presented with the trappings of power which the world recognizes and respects. For example, he was conscious that he could either preach the gospel in its stark absurdity, keeping the fact of Christ-crucified front and center, or that he could adorn it with the cosmetics which appealed to his hearers' zest for wisdom or respect for powerful signs. In choosing to preach it in its startling discontinuity from worldly wisdom and power, we have an example of Paul's decision to let God's power operate in and through his word—foolish as it would seem to many, maybe most, of his hearers. We also have an example of the limpidity of spirit which Paul himself brought to the task of being an apostle to the Gentiles, since he included himself in the seeming absurdity of proclaiming the gospel of Christ-crucified.

> For I decided to know nothing among you except Jesus Christ and him crucified. And I was with you in weakness and in much fear and trembling; and my speech and my message were not in plausible words of wisdom, but in demonstration of the Spirit and of power, that your

> faith might not rest in the wisdom of men but in the power of God. (1Cor 2,2-5)

One cannot help but be impressed by these words, as indeed by their even more startling expression in 1Cor 1,17 where Paul indicates that he was sent by Jesus to preach the gospel "not with eloquent wisdom, lest the cross of Christ be emptied of its power." Even though he knew that "the word of the cross is folly to those who are perishing" (v. 18), he nevertheless withstood the temptation to camouflage its foolishness, with the result that its wisdom came through to those who were being saved by it. In brief, Paul himself is a very good example of the understanding of the powerlessness of power (and vice versa) in the new creation. He was willing to submit his person to the humiliating fact that

> God chose what is foolish in the world to shame the wise ... what is weak in the world to shame the strong ... what is low and despised in the world ... to bring to nothing things that are, so that no human being might boast in the presnce of God. (1Cor 1,27-29)

Paul went even further. He chose to boast of his weaknesses rather than his powers. He explained to his people, for example, in 2Cor 12,7-10, that he was continually aware of his weakness because Jesus decided to leave a thorn in his flesh as if it were "a messenger of Satan, to harass me." Even though he sought to be rid of it, he was learning by accepting it that the Lord was teaching him that " 'My grace is sufficient for you, for my power is made perfect in weakness' " (v. 9). Consequently, he could confidently "boast of my weaknesses, that the power of Christ may rest upon me ... for when I am weak, then I am strong" (v. 10).

Paul also has some interesting observations about being "in positions of power" in the Church, as we in our unconverted mentalities carelessly put it. In 1Cor 4,9-13, he explains to his Christian brothers and sisters that he and all the apostles, by contrast to them, are

> as last of all, like men sentenced to death . . . we have become a spectacle to the world . . . We are fools for Christ's sake . . . weak . . . in disrepute . . . ill-clad and buffeted and homeless . . . reviled . . . persecuted . . . slandered . . . we have become, and are now, as the refuse of the world, the off-scouring of all things. (1Cor 4,9-13)

All the way through this passage he contrasts his and the other authorities' situation with the situation of his brother and sister Christians whom he sees as being in situations of honor; he sees them as blessed, he sees them as wise, strong, etc. Indeed, they have strength, wisdom, and life—by reason of Paul's sufferings. It is as if his sufferings were those of a woman in labor (Gal 4, 19) who was bringing forth others into life in Christ.

In a word, Paul experienced new life in Christ and a whole host of powers he hadn't known before; but he also experienced simultaneously a condition that he could only describe as being "crucified with Christ" (Gal 2,20). As James D. G. Dunn notes, the force of the perfect tense of the verb rather than the aorist is: "I am still in this condition. I have been nailed to Christ's own cross and I'm still hanging there."[8] Paul accepted the ongoing condition of dying which accompanied his being raised and made one with Christ; the condition of weakness so that the strength he manifested might be accurately traced to its divine source; the ongoing condition of being "in the flesh" while "in the Spirit." A life circumscribed by limitation and weakness—physical, emotional, intellectual, relational, volitional, religious, and psychological—must be accepted as an intrinsic part of what "being in the Spirit" means. Paul, while he refused to be dictated to by these limitations and weaknesses, never exhorted anyone to try to circumvent them. Life "in the flesh" was distinguished by him from "life according to the flesh." He viewed the former positively. He could "rejoice in my sufferings" because "in my flesh I complete what is lacking in Christ's afflictions for the sake of his body, that is, the church" (Col 1,24). The theological reality that undergirds this Pauline teaching is the eschatological nature of the kingdom to which we both belong and still await.

Paul, like Jesus before him, does not see the powers that God confers upon believers in the new creation as being simple additions to those enjoyed and exercised by reason of the prior gift of one's creation—that wouldn't do justice to their paschal nature. Rather, these powers come to be and gain in strength as their recipients grow in acceptance of the weakness and limitations of life in the flesh. This is tantamount to accepting one's own status as a child, God's child—dependent and powerless alone. This, in turn, makes the exercise of one's powers more likely to be directed for the benefit of others, after the manner of a servant.

The charismatic renewal must keep the paradox of power and powerlessness in balance for the sake of the witness value its example can provide for the rest of the Church, which has too often assigned privilege, rather than service, to power. It must also prevent a para-clericalism from developing in its own ranks. Finally, by living in the paradox that Jesus teaches from the throne of his cross about power, the renewal can become increasingly credible to the rest of the Church, as well as the world. Powerlessness as lived and taught by Jesus and Paul is the other half of the gospel lesson about the powers that God would bestow on us in Christ.

NOTES

1. Karl Rahner, *The Dynamic Element in the Church* (New York: Herder and Herder, 1964), p. 36.
2. Karl Rahner, "Observations on the Factor of the Charismatic in the Church," *Theological Investigations,* Vol. XII (London: Darton, Longman and Todd, 1974), p. 86.
3. Bernard Lonergan, "Dialectic of Authority," *Authority,* ed. F. Adelmann (The Hague: Martinus Nijhoff, 1974), pp. 29-30.
4. Karl Rahner, "The Teaching Office of the Church in the Present-Day Crisis of Authority," *Theological Investigations,* Vol. XII, p. 29.
5. *Ibid.,* pp. 26-28.
6. E. Schweizer, *Church Order* 21 g. Also E. Kasemann, especially his "Ministry and Community" in *Essays on New Testament Themes,* Studies in Biblical Theology, Series 41 (London: S.C.M. Press, 1964).
7. Cf. *Theological Dictionary of the New Testament,* ed. Kittel (Grand Rapids: Eerdmans Publishing Co., 1964), Vol. II, article by Grundmann on power (pp. 284-317), and by Foerster on authority (pp. 560-75).
8. James D.G. Dunn, *Jesus and the Spirit* (Philadelphia: The Westminster Press, 1975), p. 331.

A RESPONSE TO JOHN HAUGHEY'S PAPER
Bruce Yocum

Fr. Haughey initially defines charismata as "those powers manifest in individual Christians which are not traceable to the fact of office or the conferral of any powers or jurisdiction on these individuals by the Church." He then narrows the definition by considering only such "powers" as confer on individuals an ability "through their gifts to positively influence the religious, social, and moral behavior of others." That seems to me a rather restrictive approach to the charisms, since many charisms confer very little, if any, influence (e.g., tongues, healing). However, Fr. Haughey's concern is with leadership, and his choice to consider only those charisms that contribute to leadership ability is consistent with his concern.

It is notoriously difficult to provide a definition of "charisms" which is at the same time broad enough to include all that comes under this term in scripture, and precise enough to be helpful for discussion. It is common within covenant communities to use a model, however, that differs from Fr. Haughey's influence model.

In the sense employed by members of covenant communities, a "charism" is a gift (or endowment or ability) given by God to equip individuals to serve others within the Body of Christ. A "charism" enables someone to serve; the concept is therefore centered on the usefulness of the gift to others, not on its usefulness to the one who exercises it. In the New Testament, "charisms" are most often discussed in connection with the image of the body precisely because the focus of the charism is the service of the other "members."

THEOLOGICAL REFLECTIONS

The relationship between "charismatic authority" and office in the Church is complex and subtle. Many of the observations made by Fr. Haughey have some real significance, yet his concern with influence over others tends to distort the picture. Several points in particular are worth mentioning.

The model of a "fruitful tension" between those exercising charisms and those in office is of limited usefulness. Presumably this approach is based upon some physical model. But tension in human relationships, and tension between elements of a physical system are two very different things. If tension between members is not always bad, it does not seem very appealing as an *ideal*. Paul speaks of each part of the body "working together" with each other part for common growth (Eph 4,16).

Perhaps the model of fruitful tension is based upon the tension between various interest groups in a political process. But that is surely not appropriate within the Christian community, where each person is supposed to look "not only to his own interests, but also to the interests of others" (Phil 2,4). Certainly we can expect tension to develop from time to time within the community—but as a byproduct and not as a principle of organization.

The picture of officeholders and "charismatics" living in a kind of tension with one another is perhaps most justifiable if the charism considered as archetypical is prophecy. Scripture provides many colorful examples of the prophet and the king, or the prophet and the priest, at odds with one another. But even here two observations can be made. First, the tension arises when someone is doing wrong. Tension is not the fruitful result of each one doing his part. It is the unfortunate result of a failure on the part of one or the other. Second, the tension was not between "prophecy" and "office," but between two individuals. This tension was experienced by the righteous non-prophet of 600 B.C. as well as by Jeremiah. To consider such situations an instance of the tension between "charism" and "office" is to read into them the concerns of a later day.

RESPONSE

All of this is significant. The charismatic renewal claims to be a revitalization of something that has not been experienced on a wide scale in the Church for many years. In the years since charisms of the kind seen in the renewal were freely and frequently exercised, much theorizing has been done in regard to the place of charismatic gifts in the Church. But we can expect that some wrong notions have developed, too, since this theorizing has occurred in the notable absence of manifest charismatic activity. It is a serious mistake to carry over indiscriminately an understanding of charisms arrived at in the absence of charismatic activity. Rather, the new incidence of charismatic activity should be looked upon as an opportunity to recontour our thinking about charisms and their place in the life of the Church. It is a mistake to bring into the renewal a notion of their relationship to office which had developed prior to the renewal, without allowing the renewal itself to serve as the occasion of a serious reassessment.

One other point could be made in this area. Fr. Haughey comments that "charismatics might be prone to see formal authority in the Church in a negative rather than a positive light." On the contrary, at least within most covenant communities (I say "at least most covenant communities" because I am not familiar with all of them), members tend to appreciate and support those in formal authority—precisely because they have, within their communities, seen the very great benefits of well-administered formal authority. There is, however, a realization that in its relation to formal authority within the Church, the renewal is speaking from an experience with which many who hold office in the Church are simply not familiar. They too will have to take cognizance of the genuine newness of what is experienced within the renewal.

Comments on several specific points touched upon in the paper are necessary, but will have to be made very briefly.

Fr. Haughey states that "charismatic authority misinterprets its nature when it attempts to influence behavior by binding those under it to courses of action as if it were office or by taking upon itself a degree of permanence that is not assured by any charism." Presumably this is a reference to convenant communities. If so, then the assertion that charismatic authority is trying to become formal authority or office is based upon a confusion. The voluntary organization of a group into a community includes the introduction of *genuine* formal authority within the group. This step is not a matter of "charismatic authority" institutionalizing itself. Furthermore, since this step is not based upon any individual's charisms, it is not a matter of "charismatic authority" taking upon itself any "permanence."

There is a tendency, repeated in this paper, to liken covenant communities to "anabaptist" Church polity. This sort of comparison seems to me unjust both to covenant communities and to the anabaptist tradition. The statement that "the only authority in such a Church [referring to anabaptist Churches] is charismatic" is a serious misrepresentation of the anabaptist tradition. On the other hand, the implication that the experience of members of covenant communities takes place within a framework that is "revivalist, noninstitutional, privatistic" betrays a lack of familiarity with the realities of life in a covenant community.

Finally, there seems to be a confusion in Fr. Haughey's discussion of charismatic authority becoming the judge of formal authority. Fr. Haughey misses the distinction between moral judgments and pastoral judgments. Though I myself have never heard the judgments about religious orders being "unrenewable" to which Fr. Haughey refers, I do not have any difficulty seeing the possibility of such judgments being soundly-based pastoral judgments about the usefulness of a particular institutional form. Those judgments do not seem to me "unconscionable." In fact, if we are unable to ever judge (that is, use our reason to determine) that certain forms are no longer helpful, then we have lost the ability to change and respond to new circumstances.

RESPONSE

The existence of covenant communities within the Church is certainly a challenge to the Church. They can (if they remain faithful to the Spirit of God) represent today what Ignatius Loyola or Francis of Assisi or Anthony of Egypt have represented in the past—a movement within the Church which commands a wide following but which is distinct from the official leadership of the Church. The lessons of history are obvious. If both Church officials and the leaders of such communities are devoted to the good of God's people, then the movement can be successfully integrated with great benefit for all. If they are defensive or uncooperative, much good that God intends can be lost.

LIBRARY OF DAVIDSON COLLEGE